Larry McMurtry and the Victorian Novel

NUMBER FIVE
Tarleton State University
Southwestern Studies in the Humanities
William T. Pilkington, Series Editor

Larry McMurtry

AND THE VICTORIAN NOVEL

By Roger Walton Jones

Texas A&M University Press
College Station

PS
3563
A319
Z73
1994

Library of Congress Cataloging-in-Publication Data

Jones, Roger Walton, 1953–
    Larry McMurtry and the Victorian novel / by Roger Walton Jones.
        p.   cm. — (Tarleton State University southwestern studies in the
humanities ; no. 5)
    Originally presented as the author's thesis (Ph.D.) — Texas A&M University.
    Includes bibliographical references and index.
    ISBN 0-89096-621-4
    1. McMurtry, Larry — Knowledge — Literature.   2. English fiction — 19th
century — Appreciation — United States.   3. American fiction — English
influences.   I. Title.   II. Series.
PS3563.A319Z73   1994
1st ed.
813'.54 — dc20   94-15607
                                                                            CIP

This book is dedicated to Chatham Township, New Jersey,
my hometown,
and to my mother
for encouraging my love of books.

———————————

Tell me what the artist is, and I will tell you
of what he has *been* conscious.
— Henry James

Contents

Preface

I WAS ON AN AMTRAK TRAIN headed to New York when I first read *Terms of Endearment*. I had never been to Texas, but something about the way this sensitive author wrote made me care instantly about this strange place Aurora couldn't control. My train that day was headed to New York, but it might as well have been headed toward Texas, for already the spark had been lit for me concerning this unique place and its author.

In a way McMurtry and I were headed in opposite directions — though I didn't know it at the time. He had headed East even as I soon found myself accepting a teaching job in his native state. As fate would have it, when I finally returned to graduate school to get my doctorate at Texas A& M, McMurtry was already completing the novel — *Lonesome Dove* — which would earn him the Pulitzer. That prize made it easy for me to get permission to write a dissertation on him, but I was still vaguely frustrated that it took such an event to release McMurtry from the restricted label of regional writer.

From the beginning, part of my goal, therefore, was to treat McMurtry in an original way, without condescension, by focusing on those underlying thematic concerns which haunt the artist's work regardless of setting. Perhaps my undergraduate training at Kenyon College, where New Criticism once reigned, played a role in this. In any case, my surprise discovery of an early, unpublished short story entitled "Angels near the Star: A Prelude to Remembrance" became my starting point, for its poignant combination of religious yearning and frustrated spirituality provided an important look inside McMurtry's heart and soul, a window through which I would come to understand his later work. And indeed, the ways in which McMurtry himself was reflected in his subsequent work, and their connection to the author's lifelong interest in the Victorian novel, became the focus of my book. My last major chapter returns to where I began, with an in-depth look at "Angels near the Star." Ultimately, my study almost began to write itself as I investigated McMurtry's works, ranging the entire spectrum of his career. Perhaps because I found the journey so exhilarating, throughout it my attention remained more on McMurtry and his writing than on references to specific Victorian authors and their novels which may have influenced him. While some striking parallels are suggested, especially regarding Thomas Hardy and George Eliot, they are not intended to be exhaustive or even this study's first concern. Rather, as I state in my introduction, my primary purpose was to attempt to pinpoint what attracted McMurtry, a product of a distinct culture in a state of transition, to "the sense of a world" such novels convey.

One final thought. When I began this study, I wanted to de-emphasize McMurtry's links to Texas, so as to free him from regional stereotypes. Of course what I ultimately came to realize is that what made the author who he is remained intimately connected to that environment which initially both fed and rejected him. Who is to say if McMurtry had been born in an entirely different kind of setting what kind of fiction, if any, he would have been inspired to write? Such questions, however intriguing, are beyond the scope of this book.

Acknowledgments

WRITING THIS BOOK which began as a dissertation has been one of the most positive experiences of my life. This has been due in no small part to the help and guidance I received along the way.

First, I wish to thank the former head of my dissertation committee at Texas A&M, Mark Busby, who from the start encouraged me and allowed me plenty of space within which to formulate my ideas. Without such gentle nurturing, this book might never have been born. Furthermore, I wish to thank the other members of my committee, including Kenneth Price and Clinton Machann, both of whom were very generous in offering their literary insights.

I also wish to thank Henry Dan Piper, my former professor at Southern Illinois University, for his constant support over the years and for offering his reaction to an early version of this manuscript. I further wish to thank my parents, Chastine and Gloria Jones, for support both moral and financial, and especially my mother for patiently reading an early draft and providing me feedback from someone outside the profession.

I want to thank Steve Liter for helping me understand the creative process and remaining unfailingly optimistic. I am grateful to Jerome Loving and Joanna Gibson for predicting one day my manuscript would be published. I wish to thank my friend Larry Fink for taking my picture. Russell Kirk and J. H. Brown have both been an invaluable help by carefully typing my manuscript on a word processor and proofreading it closely in the process. I am indebted as well to the acquisitions editor at Texas A&M University Press, Noel Parsons, for responding so favorably to my ideas regarding McMurtry and strongly urging me to revise the manuscript for style.

Finally, I wish to thank the subject of this book, Larry McMurtry, who generously granted me permission early on to use the unpublished materials available in the Special Collections Department at the University of Houston library. I am also indebted to him for promptly responding to

Acknowledgments

my written questions regarding the influence of the Victorian novel on his work and offering me invaluable inspiration in the process. I sincerely hope my finished book in some way merits his gracious cooperation and support.

Larry McMurtry and the Victorian Novel

CHAPTER ONE

Expanding Horizons

IMAGINE IN THE FALL OF 1956 a lonely, alienated college student from Archer City writing his buddy back home that he considers life "a ball no matter how hard I try to be pessimistic."[1] Not unusual sentiments for a college boy to have. But imagine in addition that this particular young man would one day find himself winning a Pulitzer Prize and being honored by his rural hometown after mercilessly satirizing it in fiction. Such a story came true for Larry McMurtry, who has few rivals in turning youthful dreams into reality. Perhaps there is a connection between the author's impressive success and his often stated, but rarely examined, affinity for Victorian fiction.

Many times in his career, McMurtry has claimed the importance of the Victorian novel as a continued source of inspiration.[2] Once, in correspondence with me, he confirmed his extensive familiarity with Victorian novelists and mentioned two—George Eliot's *Middlemarch* and Thomas Hardy's *The Woodlanders*—as being particularly important in this regard. Speaking of Victorian novels in general, he made the interesting comment that he likes the "sense of a world" these novels convey.[3]

This book modestly sets out to explore what may be found in that "sense of a world" to attract Larry McMurtry, the individual. For, ever since the budding eighteen-year-old author sat down and wrote an intensely personal short story entitled "Angels near the Star: A Prelude to Remembrance," a moral sensibility and philosophy reminiscent of the Victorians has haunted his work.

Indeed, from the beginning, McMurtry saw the importance of a form of fiction which had as its goal something more than mere oblivion, a fiction which had as its focus interpersonal relations and civilized values.

While writing about the Beat authors for his college literary magazine, for example, the young McMurtry attacked their work for leading "logically to oblivion," and he quoted Kenneth Rexroth:

> The disengagement of the creator, who, as creator, is necessarily judge, is one thing, but the utter nihilism of the emptied out hipster is another. . . . It is impossible to go on saying "I am proud to be a delinquent," without destroying all civilized values. Between such persons, no true enduring relationships can be, and, of course, nothing resembling a true culture — an atoneness of men with each other. . . .[4]

Years later, McMurtry's concern with the moral substance of art would be reflected in a collection of nonfiction essays when he wrote:

> I have come to want more from art than either documentary authenticity or casual honesty. I have, I suspect, come to want of it what Matthew Arnold wanted: That is, that it perform a function once the trust of religion, that of reconciling us to our experience, whether social, domestic, or tragic. I want an art that — through style, through wit, through vision, or through heart — redeems the experience it presents; the last thing I want is an art that idly documents discontents and as idly adds them to my own. (*Film Flam* 44)

In his attempts to reconcile the reader to experience, and thus give his art a religious function, McMurtry was inspired by the Victorians' treatment of three major themes: the problem of reconciling the needs of the individual with those of society, the growing conflict between civilization and nature in an industrial age, and the attempt to find a basis for spirituality in a world without God or faith in organized religion.

Using these themes, McMurtry creates fiction of enormous depth and complexity. Too often due to the deceptive simplicity of his style and his mastery of traditional narrative, the high quality of McMurtry's work has been ignored or treated with condescension by literary critics charmed by the convolutions of postmodernism. This study sets out to help correct that injustice.

One of the greatest Victorian novelists, George Eliot, once wrote: "The greatest benefit we owe to the artist, whether painter, poet, or novelist, is the extension of our sympathies. . . . Art is the nearest thing to life; it is a mode of amplifying experience and extending our contract with our fellow-men beyond the bounds of our personal lot" (*Essays of George Eliot* 270–71). While many Victorian writers explored in depth the subject of friendship and its spiritual dimensions, the subject has been largely ignored by serious authors in this century. As critic Ron Sharp has pointed out, the mass mediums of television and movies are where the subject has been treated seriously.[5] Undoubtedly, part of McMurtry's success in these fields comes from the public's hunger for serious art which addresses the human need to feel connected to others. Larry McMurtry's concern with the question of how the individual may still relate to society and his anxiety over the modern dangers of solipsism recall novelists such as Eliot, Dickens, and Hardy. One of McMurtry's Washington friends has said that the author "lives through his writing" (Sweeney 16), an appropriate comment considering that through his continual fictional examination of his relation to society, his closeness to Victorian literature partly reveals itself.

Chapter 2 uses unpublished letters to explore how McMurtry's early alienation from Archer City determined the form of *The Last Picture Show*. Using it as a paradigm, I will show how the author repeatedly tempers his angry criticism of society with positive moral values provided by a few outstanding individuals who represent the author's insights with regard to men and women's highest capabilities. Suggestions of how McMurtry transforms his anxiety surrounding relationships in other novels will also be explored.

In *The Novel in the Victorian Age,* Robin Gilmour rightly argues that novels by Elizabeth Gaskell, George Eliot, William Makepeace Thackeray, and others, which create a recent past, reveal not the "objectivity of the historical novelist sitting in comfortable detachment from a past" but instead suggest something "altogether more personal and subjective, in which memory and nostalgia play their part, as well as the desire of the individual in an age of rapid change to orient himself or herself in relation to past and present by discovering, or more precisely uncovering, a sense of personal and social continuity and stability" (57–58). And Kathleen Tillotson has pointed out how this tension created by the shift from a rural to an industrial age became symbolized by the railroad for Victorian authors: "Cut off abruptly from the stagecoach world of their youth, they prolonged and idealized it" (Gilmour 59).

Driving west on the interstate from Dallas–Fort Worth, it is hard not to experience a sensation of stepping back in time. In the small, burnt-out country towns which dot the landscape, life can still be painfully slow and uncluttered, like something out of a Hardy novel. This is where McMurtry dreamed his initial dreams of a romantic cowboy past no longer available to him, dreams fueled by family stories. The author has written that, as a boy, he would "sit on the barn my uncles sat on to watch the last trail herds go by, and from there, or, as had been more common (it not being easy to climb barns), from the top of the windmill I could see a long way, into some great sunsets and far back into the mythic reaches of the West, to which . . . I could never . . . ever fail to respond" (*Film Flam* 148). And in looking back, McMurtry would feel a common sense of displacement with the Victorians, a feeling that he was a victim of an age of transition between a rural and industrial age. And like Victorian novelists, such as George Eliot and Thomas Hardy, he would attempt in fiction to reconcile nature with civilization and, thereby, achieve — with mixed results — a sense of continuity between past and present.

This desire on McMurtry's part to reconcile nature with civilization sets him apart from many American writers, including the American Transcendentalists, and helps explain his stated antipathy toward them.[6] Robert Weisbach has written: "The world really, securely, imposingly exists for the Englishman. It is chiefly mysterious, portable, wispy, and insecure for the American" (105). The world of culture associated with Europe and the potential open-minded tolerance for diverse points of view greatly attracted McMurtry, coming, as he did, from a highly provincial fundamentalist town in which books were scarce. It is not, therefore, surprising that he might, with sensitivity and intelligence, defend Arnold's faith in "the best that is known and thought in the world" (268) or that the tangible world of social relations revealed in Victorian novels might attract him over the poetic musings of metaphysical transcendentalists.

Chapter 3 explores the author's complex, often highly ambivalent responses to both civilization and nature. For, despite his early attraction to culture, McMurtry would later long to return to nature. This conflict, never fully resolved, helps inspire his most famous work, *Lonesome Dove,* the novel which forms the chapter's central focus.

In *The Victorian Fame of Mind,* Walter Houghton explains how writers like George Eliot "adopted a secular ethic of enthusiasm to save the moral foundations of society in an age of doubt" (272). This idea, inherited from the Romantics, involved "that higher state of mind, in which selfish desires of the ego, far from having to be conquered by the moral will, are swept aside by the selfless impulse of the 'noble' emotions, in a state of enthusiasm. And though in itself ephemeral, it has lasting effects" (263–64). Despite his early alienation and moments of despair, McMurtry's fiction includes moments of special reconciliation and inspiration which recall the Victorian ethic of enthusiasm.

Chapter 4 explores the author's use of such moments, moments in which he temporarily overcomes his solipsism and the past tensions which continue to haunt him. My chapter begins with a close look at an early, unpublished short story which contains one such moment as it puts the themes already mentioned in a religious context. In a world lacking religious faith, people turn more than ever to nature, and especially civilization and society, in their search for something transcendent. In such a world, McMurtry characters opt for Wordsworthian moments which affirm the existence of a realm beyond the merely finite and temporal and which facilitate an ideal balance between civilization and nature, between society and the individual.

One such moment came to life in 1986, the year the author won the Pulitzer Prize. In that year, the once painfully lonely boy found himself honored by his hometown of Archer City. In his acceptance speech, McMurtry managed to gracefully pay respect to the place, so indelibly a part of him, which he ironically had put so much effort into moving beyond:

> I have to tell you that this award moves me more and surprises me more than winning the Pulitzer Prize. It's one thing to write a book that appeals to the taste of the people on the prize committee. It's harder to earn the respect of people who know you. The myth is that small towns in America don't care about their writers and are small minded and intolerant. But here I am, a writer being honored by his hometown. In a sense, you have all helped me with this award. I don't know if I have ever used a literal event that has happened in this town, but what I have used are the intimations and hunches you have given me.[7]

A sense of having come full circle, of having momentarily reconciled feelings associated with people and place, time and space, must have hung in the air. Surely it couldn't last. But standing in Archer City that afternoon, McMurtry, nonetheless, should have been proud.

CHAPTER TWO

The Last Picture Show

THE RELATION OF THE INDIVIDUAL TO SOCIETY

The terrible insistencies of society — how severe they are, and cold, and inexorable — ghastly towards those who are made of wax and not of stone. O, I am afraid of them; a stab for this error, and a stab that — correctives and regulations pretendly framed that society may tend to perfection — an end which I don't care for in the least. Yet for this all I do care for has to be stunted and starved.

—Thomas Hardy, *The Woodlanders*

"SOMETIMES SONNY FELT like he was the only human creature in the town" — so opens *The Last Picture Show,* a novel, like so many by Larry McMurtry, filled with the palpable ache of loneliness. Yet with this, his third novel, McMurtry would for the first time attempt to assuage the pain of social isolation by an exploration of society and, in the process, open doors to possible avenues of reconciliation. In contrast to his first novel, his protagonist would, ultimately, choose not to escape from, but to confront, his social demons.

J. Hillis Miller has aptly pointed out how the great Victorian novelists, such as Charles Dickens, William Makepeace Thackeray, George Eliot, Anthony Trollope, George Meredith, and Thomas Hardy, all began from positions of social isolation from which they examined the question of individual authenticity, as well as the authenticity of the community (*The Form of Victorian Fiction* 94). McMurtry's use of this dual process signaled a step forward for him as an artist. Like George Eliot and Thomas Hardy, he would find himself rejecting the traditional Christianity of his heritage, intensifying his focus on alternative ways the individual may seek transcendence. And further echoing these two prominent Victorians, the author would remain an outsider in spirit, even as he moved in circles of the successful and elite.

The college letters McMurtry wrote his friend Mike Kunkel reveal important clues as to the genesis of his third novel and its relation to his personal concerns. They suggest a highly thoughtful, sensitive young man, extremely serious but nonetheless possessed of great humor. Additionally, they convey a young man fascinated with culture and unable to accept a dogmatic, conformist Christianity which does not allow for questioning. Finally, they reflect a man at times painfully torn between his marked concern for others and his need to define himself as an individual. In a letter dated August 31, 1956, McMurtry wrote:

> You can't imagine how horrible it is to be the least bit different from your provincial fellow man. I have dropped church from my curricular [*sic*] until the day when a Unitarian one comes near, largely because I was becoming increasingly choked on the Apostles Creed, and I may be burned at the stake any day now. The folks are bad, but other people are worse behind my back. They plague Maxwell continually about my atheism, which is absurd. They can not comprehend that a person can not be a Meth. Christian, and still a theist. I am passive, but waiting for an opening in which to thrust with knife like wit.[1]

And in another letter dated January 24, 1956, McMurtry declared:

> Archer City is rather a mess. If I didn't love the place I'd hate it violently. A bunch of almost inextricably mixed up kids. . . . I am oftimes [*sic*] on the verge of schizophrenia and the rest can shove off for Hell anytime, except a few choice adults. All the rest are utter chaos. Lenn is regrettably but undeniably frigid, Jeter is a pretty shell, Anne the other has sunk plumb out of sight, and damn near took Mary with her, Lonnie Wilson is lovable, but in love with a girl whose folks are in their estimation to [*sic*] good for him.

Behind such brief comments on the people he knew from Archer City, one can already see the formation of character types which would lay the foundation for *The Last Picture Show*. The words "regrettably but undeniably frigid" could easily apply to Ruth; "a pretty shell," to Jacy; and "in love with a girl whose folks are too good for him," to Duane. Significant too is the respect reserved for "a few choice adults," as the strongest, most admirable characters in the novel will be older people. Also noteworthy is his self-description of being "on the verge of schizophrenia," as his third novel would be highly ambivalent in tone.

In a letter dated June 17, 1957, McMurtry angrily sums up the people of Archer City as "drags (a surprisingly useful word which, in this case, encompasses prudes, bigots, hypocrites, cretins, snobs, illiterates, ad infinitum)." Yet, however strident and petulant McMurtry's tone is at times in relation to the town he would outgrow, there remains in the to-be-famous writer a lonely vulnerability and genuine concern for others. For example, in an earlier letter, postmarked November 11, 1956, he writes his friend, "I am afoot, or I would come and see you most every weekend. I sure wish you were down here, because I have no one to talk to who has more than a superficial knowledge of most things I like to talk about." Along with the letter, he includes a poignant series of questions and answers which underscore his social pain and fear of loss. In answer to one question he asks himself (What would you like to do, to know, to be, in case [*sic*] you aren't satisfied?"), he replies in part that he would "like to live where I could do as I see fit without bringing consternation to people whom I care for, but do not think some of the things I do are fit." In answer to another question ("What do you fear most from the future?"), McMurtry answers, "Loneliness, that impending financial insolvency will make me abandon ambition in favor of security, the death of people I care for deeply." And in another letter, dated September 30, 1955, with reference to a friend who has dropped out of college, the author writes, "Jim was mostly homesick they say. There, I sympathize heartily, for that can be a very sick sick."

Besides McMurtry's specific ambivalence in relation to Archer City and his alienation from its fundamentalist religion, hints of another important form of alienation appear in his letters which would influence his fiction long after his anger over organized religion was no longer a major factor. It involves the personal emptiness which results from being defined neither as a cowboy nor a sophisticate, but a perennial outsider. In the author's first published collection of nonfiction essays, *In a Narrow Grave,* he would candidly admit his early inability to fit the ranching mode:

> With most of my uncles I had no rapport at all. To their practiced eye it must have been evident from the first that I was not going to turn out to be a cattleman. For one thing, I wasn't particularly mean, and in the West the mischief quotient is still a popular standard for measuring the appearance of approving masculine qualities in a youngster. Any boy worth his salt was expected to be a nuisance, if not to the adults at least to weaker members of his own age group. I was a weaker member myself; indeed, though I don't remember it, I believe at some early and very primitive reunion I was cast

into a hog wallow or pelted with ordure or something; though the atrocity may be apocryphal it would not have been out of keeping with the spirit of such occasions.

Because of their important connection to the replayed role of social misfit or outsider as victim in his fiction, McMurtry's childhood recollections here are worth quoting at length:

> Mean kids mean strength in time of need, and how could the elders be sure that a bookish and suspiciously observant youngster like myself might not in time disgrace the line? I knew from an early age that I could never meet their standard, and since in those days theirs was the only standard I knew existed I was the more defensive around them. Indeed, scared. One was mild and two were gentle; the rest, with one exception, were neither harder nor softer than saddle leather. The one exception, was, in my estimation, harder than your average saddle leather. Tolerance was a quality I think no McMur- try ever understood, much less appreciated, and though one or two of them came to understand mercy it was not the family's long suit. (158–59)

The good news here is that McMurtry's fear and anger in response to the simplistic masculine intolerance he felt as a child in rural Texas would later inspire him to create fiction which celebrated not only women but toler- ance as a positive quality associated with civilization. Like many Victorian novelists, including Charles Dickens, McMurtry's strong feelings of being set apart from his peers due to circumstances beyond his control would lead to a fiction of reconciliation.

On the other hand, like Thomas Hardy, the author would view with habitual distrust and ambivalence the sophisticated world of the so-called successful, a world he would increasingly enter, though perhaps never fully feel part of, as he became famous.[2] As early as his college days, he would look on success with suspicion and a sense of loss. In a letter dated October 20, 1955, for example, McMurtry writes, "Gee Mike, you don't know how much I miss you. You are my sane rational person who isn't so enmeshed in a gold plated veneer of scholasticism that they can't see out." And in another letter, dated December 3 of the same year, he wrote,

> I'm more of a social agnostic than anything, because I despise social or intel- lectual elite to such a terrifying degree. I want no part of that kind of brains or that kind of money. As friend Maugham says, culture's only yardstick is character. What profits it to have read a thousand books or to have plowed a thousand fields if it has done nothing but make you look down on those who haven't.

McMurtry's admirable refusal to hide his rural heritage or diminish his values as he became part of the sophisticated literary art world would form the basis for the conflict between civilization and nature in his fiction, a conflict explored most fully in the next chapter.

Before McMurtry would be able to treat that conflict with equanimity, however, he would find himself first exorcising rural ghosts. In McMurtry's first two novels, *Horseman, Pass By* and *Leaving Cheyenne,* the young author's first person narrators capture both his original alienation and lingering nostalgia regarding his ranching heritage. But with his third novel, *The Last Picture Show,* in which he confronted his more recent high school experience, Larry McMurtry's considerable capacity for anger found its greatest expression.

If *The Last Picture Show* was notable for that, and nothing more, it would not merit extensive discussion. But far from being a mere angry outburst, it signaled a significant turning point in the author's artistic growth. Here, for the first time, he broadened his scope to depict a wide variety of characters who form a particular society in miniature. Here, also for the first time, he found an all-knowing, seemingly objective narrator who moves among the inhabitants of a small town in a time of cultural transition, mixing satire with realism, criticism with affection. In this respect, its overall plan would loosely recall George Eliot's famous novel *Middlemarch,* one of McMurtry's favorites.

J. Hillis Miller has eloquently described the narrative voice of Victorian novelists as one which "surrounds and permeates each individual human mind and therefore is able to know it perfectly from the inside, to live its life" (64), and the same words could effectively describe McMurtry's insightful narrative voice in *The Last Picture Show.* While the author's variation of tone at times suggests a lack of distance from his material, a close examination of his novel nonetheless shows that his mix of satire and realism serves to effectively underscore his moral purpose.

Before beginning that examination, however, a further mention of *Middlemarch* may prove instructive. Themes which McMurtry shares with Eliot, and which are developed in both novels, include the positive influence individuals can have on the lives of those around them when they act in ways which acknowledge social responsibility. Furthermore, both novels reveal the influence of Wordsworth in their stress upon an individual's search for the spiritual unity which lies behind life's varied, seemingly unrelated moments. And in relation to this poignant search, both authors dramatize the conflict between a young dreamer's naive idealism and adult reality.[3]

At the center of McMurtry's dramatization of these moral issues stands Ruth Popper. Much attention has been paid by critics, such as Charles Peavy, to the importance of Sam the Lion as an authority figure and Sonny's story of sexual initiation.[4] Not enough attention, however, has been placed on Ruth Popper's role and her impressive growth in stature, which is the most pronounced in the novel. The author's straightforward tone heightens the reader's positive yet unsentimental response to Ruth's courage and humanity. Her hollow marriage to the emotionally stunted Coach Popper makes her an expert on the relation of the individual to society. Her self-awareness and simple honesty regarding her personal regeneration shine through when, after making love with Sonny, she tells him:

> Loneliness is like ice. After you've been lonely long enough you don't even realize you're cold, but you are. It's like I was a refrigerator that had never been defrosted at all—never. . . . You can't melt all that ice in a few days, I don't care how good a man you are. I didn't even realize it, like I didn't realize till now just how ugly this room is. I don't know, maybe at the center of me there's some ice that never will melt, maybe it's just been there too long. But you mustn't worry. You didn't put it there. (102)

Ruth foreshadows her potential for growth when, early on, she informs Sonny that her isolation results from a failure of initiative, a clear sign of her willingness to take responsibility for her fate: "The reason I'm so crazy is because nobody cares about me either. It's my own fault though—I haven't found the guts to do anything about it" (50).

Ruth does find the "guts," though, and reaches out to others. In the process, she becomes a living example of the potential for the individual to become a source of inspiration to others in a society lacking transcendental values. It should come as no surprise, therefore, that she is given the novel's last scene in which she comforts Sonny following Billy's death or that her first kiss with Sonny occurs approximately one-third of the way into the story (18), providing an important spiritual counterpoint to the devastation caused by Sam the Lion's sudden death about two-thirds of the way through (220). Because of the symbolic importance of the earlier scene, in which Ruth and Sonny first establish both physical and spiritual contact, to the rest of the novel, it merits careful examination.

In situation, detail, and tone, the scene resembles one which McMurtry wrote for a highly revealing, though never published, college short story entitled, "Angels near the Star: A Prelude to Remembrance" (discussed at length in Chapter 4). In the story, a boy is sitting in a church apart from others, reaching a state of private ecstasy as he allows his ample imagination free reign. He imagines many things, but the final culminating scene describes a boy and girl on a summer night who together, through love, create a Wordsworthian transcendent moment which hints at a spiritual realm beyond the merely physical:[5]

> . . . t'was a cool clean night with few stars and two of the few cast their reflection in a girl's eyes and their sparkle in the dark car was like a scattered frost in a duckhunting dawn . . . and the boy and the girl alone . . . and after a long embrace, her head resting on his shoulder . . . and she looked backward through kiss closed eyes out the back window. . . .
>
> . . . And he said, "What do you see back there?"
> . . . "A stray dog"
> "and what's his name"
> "Pooch"
> "And what else," he murmured against a soft throat.
> "a street"
> "and what's its name?"
> "Plum"
> "and what else"
> "A star"
> "just one?"
> "and what's its name"
> "Twinkle"
>
> . . . And he thought that soft word he'd felt and heard was exquisitely Beautiful, and thanked the star and the angels near it for being a "Twinkle" . . . then the moment, gone, and gone, oh gone thence forever, but left was faith that time would bring hence more. . . . And he thought its faith that God will ever bring such beauties and such Good that faith by which ye shall live alone. . . . (5, 6)

McMurtry's maturation as an artist is illustrated by the contrast between the blatant optimism displayed in the "Angels" passage versus his far more subtle handling of Sonny and Ruth's encounter in *The Last Picture Show*. The open sentimentality is muted by irony in the latter version, created in part by the author's introduction of the unromantic act of taking out the garbage:

> When they had dumped the cups into one of the barrels, Ruth hesitantly came close to Sonny and then came very close. Her cheek was warm against his throat, and he smelled the thin, clean smell of her perfume. For a minute they were too silent—Sonny looked over her head, beyond the town. Far across the pastures he saw the lights of an oil derrick, brighter than the cold winter stars. Suddenly Mrs. Popper lifted her head and they kissed. Their mouths didn't hit just right at first and she put her fingers gently on each

side of his face and guided his mouth to hers. The touch of her cool fingers startled and excited him and he pulled her to him more tightly. Her breath was warm against his cheek. Near the end of the kiss she parted her lips and teeth for a moment and touched him once with her tongue. Then she took her mouth away for several minutes and pressed her lips tightly against his throat. . . .

"Maybe we're going to have something after all," Ruth said. "Will you drive me to the hospital again next week, if I arrange for Herman to take you?"

"You bet," Sonny said. "The sooner the better, as far as I'm concerned." He bent down to find her mouth and Ruth put her hands on his cheeks again. They kissed slowly and luxuriously. At first the kiss was as soft as the first one had been, but then Ruth discovered that Sonny had awakened and was thrusting at her, not so much with his mouth as with himself, wanting more of her. He kissed her so hard her head was pushed back and when she opened her eyes for a moment she was looking straight up, towards the stars. (81, 82)

Perhaps the most striking similarity between the two scenes is McMurtry's depiction of Ruth literally looking heavenward at the stars in a moment of hopeful ecstasy. However, while the male lover in "Angels" shares his lover's faith and optimism, Ruth's sense of hope is juxtaposed against Sonny's ominous focus on the lights of the oil derrick, which appear to him "brighter" than the stars. Though the scene overall is more earthbound than the earlier one, it still portrays a transcendent moment in the lives of the characters, which serves as a welcome antidote to the alienation and loneliness that elsewhere permeate the novel.

With the next chapter, Ruth grows in strength as her search for the transcendent continues, displaying a generosity, courage, and self-awareness that other characters lack. She changes from one so obsessed with fear of her neighbors hearing her make love with Sonny that she cannot enjoy it, to a character who, by chapter's end, can brush off any fear of her husband's finding out. Instrumental to her transformation is her Wordsworthian search for "the beautiful thing . . . the whole moment towards which all sharp little individual moments tended." The narrator informs the reader that this moment was something "she had read about" (101). What Ruth discovers is that her dream of the "beautiful thing" in relation to another which assures continuity and meaning cannot be artificially manufactured or forced. When she finally fully responds to Sonny sexually, it comes as a natural outgrowth of her own inspired dreams of him as the child she never had.

In contrast to Ruth, when McMurtry writes about Jacy, Sonny's dream girl, he adopts a satiric tone which rivals William Makepeace Thackeray's treatment of Becky Sharp in *Vanity Fair.* It is this tone which serves to underscore the novel's moral purpose. For, while Ruth's sensitivity and intelligence enable her to appreciate the value of the natural and spontaneous, Jacy can only appreciate artificially contrived moments during which she is the center of attention and in control. As Charles Peavy has written, she is "narcissistic in her lovemaking, which always has the aura of a theatrical performance with herself as the star" (119). And nothing thrills her more than exploiting Duane to maximize her popular sexy image:

> She thought the light was very romantic and suggestive: everyone in the bus could tell when the couple in the back seat were kissing or doing something sexy, but the light wasn't strong enough for them to see all too clearly. Courting Duane when all the kids on the school bus could watch gave Jacy a real thrill, and made her feel a little like a movie star: she could bring beauty and passion into the poor kids' lives." (62)

The moral distance between Ruth and Jacy suggests the pattern of light and dark characters which forms the novel's backbone, giving it depth. Like George Eliot in *Middlemarch,* McMurtry uses as his canvas a small town in a time of cultural transition from a simpler to a more complex, impersonal age. The inhabitants of the town have generational incompatibilities arising over issues of selfishness versus generosity and the determination to hide behind self-serving illusions versus the willingness to deal, when necessary, with reality. McMurtry's own early alienation and ambivalence concerning these issues propel the novel and its underlying sociological concerns. Without becoming didactic, the opposition of Ruth and Jacy as respective examples of sympathy and honesty versus self-absorption and phoniness is, likewise, mirrored in the opposition of Sam the Lion and Coach Popper, in Genevieve and Charlene, in Mrs. Farrow and her daughter Jacy. The social importance of these oppositions is dramatized by Sonny's plight as he bounces back and forth between them, between feelings of personal authenticity and belonging versus emptiness and alienation. Without consciously realizing why, essentially parentless Sonny is instinctively drawn to elders like Sam the Lion, Genevieve, and Ruth, or innocents like Billy, for they alone satisfy his spiritual hunger for feelings of worth as an individual. His youthful inability to consciously discern between the natural aura of a Genevieve and the phony image of a Jacy, combined with the reader's realization that Thalia's harsh reality expands the desire for illusion, provides the novel with much of its distinctive power to move and instruct.

Just as they do in George Eliot's *Middlemarch,* women ultimately fare better than men in the search for love and honesty.[6] The immaturity of Jacy aside, it is Ruth, Genevieve, and Mrs. Farrow who bravely continue to affirm the social ties on which the humanity of society rests. And despite his mythic stature, aging Sam the Lion is seen mostly reacting rather than acting throughout the story, as in his most powerful scene when he bans the boys from the pool hall after they exploit Billy. Significantly, it is Genevieve who brings Sam and Sonny back together. Furthermore, it is, ironically, the hard-drinking Mrs. Farrow who not only visits the pathetically repressed Joe Bob in prison, but stands up for Sonny when he is abused by her dishonest daughter.

Despite these sane gestures on the part of self-aware individuals, McMurtry realistically shows how — in a small town where religion has been largely reduced to rigid social conformity — most people are too scared and ignorant to give up their convenient religious and sexual icons even when they distort the truth. Therefore, reality bearers such as Ruth and Mrs. Farrow sacrifice approval by the majority of Thalia's citizens. When Mrs. Farrow sympathizes with Joe Bob, the narrator makes clear that no one in town will listen, even if it means the needless destruction of a young individual: "'That poor kid's downfall started the day the old man Blanton got the call to preach,' Lois Farrow said, but she was the only one who took that view. No one else thought of blaming Brother Blanton for his son's disgrace, and still less did they think of blaming Coach Popper or the school board president or San Francisco or Esther Williams, the movie star" (164). Similarly, when Ruth visits Mr. Cecil, she is, ironically, confronted by an educated man so cowed by mindless social prejudice that he willingly abdicates his responsibility to question the reputation of the one who caused his downfall.

> "But *you* didn't mess it up," Ruth said. "My husband messed it up. I'll never forgive him for it. If anybody needed to be fired for . . . what they fired you for, it was him.
>
> John Cecil looked at her with astonishment. "Oh, you don't mean that, Ruth," he said, after a moment. "Why Herman's the football coach."
>
> She saw that he didn't believe her, and knew that Herman had been right. Nobody, not even John Cecil, would believe her, and in truth she didn't even know for sure herself what Herman was. She just felt sad and uncertain and wanted to cry. (156)

In such an unpromising social environment, Sonny must find his way to truth. In *The Novel in the Victorian Age,* Robin Gilmour rightly lists the

two characteristics of the Victorian bildungsroman, or novel of develop-
ment, as "the superiority of the 'real' to the 'Ideal'," and "the redemptive
power of human love" (17). Sonny's traditional story of initiation involves
his learning to accept the ordinary reality of unselfish love, which can alone
lead to transcendence over his artificially easy dream of Jacy. His quest for
fulfillment in this way echoes Dorothea's similar quest in *Middlemarch*,
which finds resolution in her acceptance of ordinary love, symbolized by
her marriage to Will Ladislaw, over impressive appearances. It resembles
as well Jude's elusive search for personal peace in *Jude the Obscure* in that
Sonny's growth is repeatedly undercut, not only by his own foibles, but
by circumstances beyond his control. In this way, McMurtry reminds the
reader not only of the failure of the town's fundamentalist religion, but
of any set of commonly held transcendent values to which the individual
may turn.

Charles Peavy oversimplifies Sonny's story of initiation when he asserts
that it is through "the medium of sex that the inhabitants of Thalia seek
(and find) their identity" (53). For in point of fact, McMurtry shows how
many *lose* their identity by linking sexual desire with what society expects
of them. Jacy is a prime example of this, for while she loses her virginity
and even contrives a mock marriage, nothing indicates that she graduates
beyond sexual stereotypes and viewing sex as a performance to gratify a
phony self-image. As the son of the town's overly repressive minister,
Joe Bob experiences such a high degree of confusion that he resorts to
a regressive cry for help which takes the form of kidnapping a little girl.
In contrast to such pathetic behavioral extremes, McMurtry shows how
reliance upon genuine caring and love, such as that displayed by Ruth,
makes sex a true component of maturation and joy, which allows one
to discover an authentic adult identity—free of the need for approval
by others.

Sonny's moral quest may begin with Ruth, but the spiritual emptiness
of his daily life in Thalia is clearly established in the novel's opening lines.
Just the look of the town in early morning with its deserted, windswept
streets evokes a barren landscape as drearily opposed to human aspiration
as Thomas Hardy's famous description of Egdon Heath which opens *The
Return of the Native*.[7] Like many Victorian protagonists, Sonny is essentially
an orphan, for he is without a mother and estranged from his father. For
these reasons the pool hall and the picture show, which Sam the Lion
bought after the death of his three sons, are especially vital sources of communal cultural experience. The importance of movie theaters to small
towns, McMurtry has suggested, lay in the fact that they "provided a con-

tinuous feed-in of discussable experience that could be balanced against that generated by the town itself . . . [movies provided] the leaven of escape; a chance to be drawn into an experience not generated by the family, the neighborhood, or the town" (*Film Flam* 103–104). Appropriately, Billy, the retarded boy and the town's natural outcast, is most closely associated with the theater. Not only does he see every movie, but he was actually conceived in the theater when "a deaf and dumb girl who had no people but an aunt" was raped (8). Because of his childlike dependence on the theater as a home and source of identity in contrast to the empty, hostile reality he would otherwise be left with, Billy is the novel's most powerful symbol of culture's crucial role as a source of inspiration for the less fortunate.

The downside of movies in McMurtry's third novel arises from the dangerous role they can play in contributing to the inability to distinguish fantasy from reality. When Sonny takes Charlene to the movies early in the novel, for example, each imagines more ideal partners: one real and one imagined via Hollywood (19–21). While Sonny dreams of Jacy and Ginger Rogers, Charlene dreams of Duane and Steve Cochran. Fantasy and reality weave in and out so often that reality appears stranger and harsher than it would otherwise. When Sonny hands Charlene back the snapshot of her in a swimsuit, the narrator informs the reader that despite her writing "Look what Legs!" on the back of it, "the photograph showed clearly that her legs were short and fat, but in spite of it she managed to think of herself as possessing gazellelike slimness" (24).

The movies, which serve as such a powerful form of escape for Sonny and his friends, are a poor substitute for the breakdown of rural values in the novel. Sonny's moral conflict underscores the replacement of a rural economy based on hard work and a closeness to nature by one based on shallow oil profits. In the third chapter, he intuitively realizes that Genevieve is a down-to-earth woman with self-awareness who stands in stark contrast to the superficiality of Jacy's appeal:

> Gallons of hot water poured into the sink and working over it soon had her sweating. Her cheeks and forehead shone with it; there were beads on her upper lip and the armpits of her green uniform darkened. The errant strand of hair hung over her forehead when she bent to fish the knives and forks out of the water. As always, Sonny found himself strongly affected by her. Sweat, if it was Genevieve's, seemed a very intimate and feminine moisture. Even Jacy didn't affect him quite as strongly; beside Genevieve, Jacy seemed strangely diminished, and apparently Jacy knew it. She always made Duane take her to the drive-in rather than the cafe when they ate together. (28)

Note the fertility implied by her bending to "fish" the utensils from the water. Appropriately, in the same scene, Genevieve mentions that ever since Jacy's parents had their oil strike, she had not seen much of them, for "when folks get rich all of a sudden it makes them feel sort of guilty to be around folks who've stayed poor" (29).

The inhumanity which new money can create in its establishment of a social elite is reflected both in Sam the Lion's warnings to the love-struck Duane and in the portrayal of Jacy and her mother as the novel progresses. Explaining to Duane that Jacy's parents want her to marry for money, Sam the Lion discourages him from living for money himself, declaring, "once you got rich you'd have to spend all your time staying rich, and that's hard and thankless work" (52). Just as the poor but faithful Giles loses his chance to marry Grace due to her socially ambitious parents in Hardy's *The Woodlanders,* so Duane ultimately loses Jacy. In contrast to Jacy's spoiled behavior is the enigmatic example set by her mother. Blessed with self-awareness and memories of harder financial times, she realizes that being rich in Thalia is "a good way to go insane" (42). Like the wealthy but frustrated Mrs. Charmond in *The Woodlanders,* whose sad words introduce this chapter, Lois copes by at times exploiting her social position. At the town party, for example, she drinks and outrageously flirts at the expense of others' wives (72). Yet, by novel's end, it is she who visits Joe Bob in jail and, following the rejection by her daughter, she who attempts to rebuild Sonny's confidence. Before going to bed with him, she states, "'You're scared of me because I'm Lois Farrow. . . . I'm rich and mean, all that. What everybody thinks of me. But that's not true for you. I may be that way with a lot of men because that's what they want and deserve, but it's still not true'" (200). After making love to him, she wisely advises, "It's not how much you're worth to a woman. . . . It's how much you're worth to yourself. It's what you really can feel that makes you nice" (201).

Lois Farrow also tells Sonny at one point that his relationship with Ruth Popper "sounded like a good thing to me" (197). The importance of Sonny's affair with Ruth and its relation to his slow and painful awakening to moral maturity are underscored in the scene following their first kiss, during which his increased psychological integration is tested:

> It had something to do with Mrs. Popper, though he was not certain just what. It didn't seem right to kiss Mrs. Popper and still fiddle around with heifers, blind or not blind. Not only did it not seem right: it no longer seemed like fun. Kissing Mrs. Popper even once was bound to be more fun than anything he could possibly do with the skinny, quivering little heifer. He suddenly had the feeling he had graduated and it was an uneasy feeling. (86)

Clearly, Mrs. Popper has been instrumental in making Sonny suddenly see the important distinction to be made between lust and love, between literally exploiting a helpless blinded animal to satisfy oneself and merging with another human being on an emotional, as well as physical, level. The fact that the heifer is blind symbolically foreshadows Sonny's own victimization and partial blindness in the novel as a result of a pointless fight over Jacy, as well as the blindness caused Billy as a result of wearing Sonny's eye patch, a blindness which contributes to his accidental death.[8]

Sonny's dawning moral and spiritual awareness makes the next episode extremely painful to him, when Duane and the other boys come up with the cruel idea of making the retarded Billy have sex with the town whore. Sonny starts to object but is too weak to assert himself as an individual: "Sonny quit arguing — he really didn't know how to argue against a whole crowd. He had never wanted to before" (87). Following the shameful incident, it is significant that Sonny guiltily waits for Sam the Lion even though he knows Sam will be angry (unlike the immature younger boys who imagine Sam might be persuaded to view it humorously). He even presents Sam with Billy's underwear when Sam asks for it, though he knows it makes him seem "more a participant than he had been" (91). Such gestures demonstrate that Sonny is painfully learning, through the discovery of love, the importance of moral responsibility to others.

Sonny's lessons in humanity are temporarily thwarted by fear and a lingering inability to distinguish reality from fantasy. That night, as he lays in bed, he experiences "a few old images of Jacy" slipping in even as he tries to recall Ruth's "face and the touch of her lips" (93). When, halfway into the novel, Jacy decides to manipulate Sonny to help distance herself from Duane, Sonny is ironically vulnerable due to the pain caused by personal growth: "He wasn't sure that he wanted any person to be his: it made him too responsible" (114).

Sam the Lion's death two-thirds of the way into the novel largely destroys what little positive sense of community Thalia has to support its young, including Sonny. Death destroys life's illusions for an individual, as it cannot be controlled or manipulated to reflect one's ego, leaving only the reality, if one is lucky, of those who truly care. Therefore, when Sonny unconsciously falls under Jacy's egocentric spell, which in turn leads to his abandonment of Ruth, he foreshadows the deaths of Sam the Lion and Billy, for he has betrayed the source of meaning upon which modern civilization depends.

Shortly before Sam the Lion's death, McMurtry solidifies the importance of Sam's role in Sonny's life by describing an afternoon they spend together fishing. Critics, such as D. Gene England have rightly stressed the significance of the scene by the stock tank as one involving male initiation in which Sam plays the traditional role of father or wise elder.[9] Certainly it is this, but it is also striking how little positive strength or wisdom Sam actually provides. Though he tells Sonny regarding Ruth that he might as well "stay with her and get some good out of her" while he's growing up and that being "crazy about a woman like her's always the right thing to do," he also tells him, "I never know what to do about anybody, least of all women." And when the easily influenced Sonny asks, "Is growing up always miserable?", Sam blithely replies, "About eighty percent of the time, I guess" (124–25).

Sam the Lion passes away while Sonny ironically is on a regressive trip to Mexico with Duane in search of whores. Yet Sonny does not have sex with the whore he sleeps beside, for she is already pregnant, and in a moment of shameful self-realization, he understands "why Ruth had insisted they make love on the floor: the cot springs wailed and screamed and made him feel as though every move he made was sinful. He had driven five hundred miles to get away from Thalia, and the springs took him right back, made him feel exposed" (139).

Thomas Landess has criticized McMurtry's introduction of a student trip to San Francisco in the chapter following Sonny's receiving news of Sam the Lion's death. He refers to Sam as Sonny's "one dependable link with the adult world" and declares that his reaction "could have been the most vital scene in the book" (*Larry McMurtry* 77). But in so doing, Landess overlooks the fact that Ruth, Genevieve, and Lois Farrow are in some ways more important role models for Sonny than Sam the Lion. Furthermore, Landess may have Sonny confused with Lonnie in *Horseman, Pass By*. Lonnie's detailed reaction to his grandfather's death, described in Chapter 4, is heightened by his superior intelligence and poetic sensibility, qualities which the athletic Sonny lacks. Finally, Landess ignores the symbolic passing of Sam's ghost, which underscores his role as a moral guide. While Sonny is still in Mexico, he comes upon an old man with white hair, like Sam's, who provides him with water from a tin dipper, a gesture with religious overtones:

> When he passed where Sonny was kneeling the old man nodded to him kindly and gestured with a tin dipper he had in his hand. Sonny gratefully took a dipper of water from him, using it to wash the sour taste out of his mouth. The old man smiled at him sympathetically and said something in a philosophic tone, something which Sonny took to mean life was a matter of ups and downs. (140)

Landess might further note what the old Mexican's words imply, namely that success in life is largely a question of being able to effectively juxtapose opposites. For the variations of narrative tone and character situation are part of McMurtry's intentional way of dramatizing the seeming meaninglessness of modern life, which he uses to heighten the meaningful moments created by positive loving relationships between individuals. That is part of the reason why, for example, he follows the sublime moment of Sonny's first kiss with Ruth with the scene where the boys copulate with the heifer and then set Billy up with a whore; or why it is appropriate that Sonny should be seeking out pornography and whores in Mexico when Sam dies. Such contrasting scenes illustrate that for McMurtry, the physical world with all its joys, frustrations, and temptations is always inextricably linked with the beauty of the spiritual. In a college letter which McMurtry wrote on November 18, 1956, he described coming upon a little boy in a bookstore "who sat on the filthy floor and sang . . . in an amazingly fine, sweet voice" until his mother "came over and started beating him with a big book." McMurtry commented, "Everytime you see something pretty like that you find something stinkin' close by."

The conclusion of the novel ties together the themes discussed in a unified way that challenges Landess' suggestion that the novel is "like an impressionist painting with a group of discrete incidents dotting in the larger image" (26). While it is true that the novel's structure is episodic in the tradition of Hardy and that its tone alternates between realism and satire, hanging over Sonny's initiation is the spirit of Ruth Popper, who exemplifies the potentially positive role the individual in society can play. So when Sam the Lion passes away, followed by Billy, it is naturally Ruth and the reality she represents which Sonny must finally face up to, for the illusions of Jacy (or even the picture show) can no longer disguise the truth. Upon attending with Duane a showing of *The Kid From Texas,* the emotional risks are clearly felt: "They had been at the picture show so often with Jacy that it was hard to keep from thinking of her . . . Such thoughts were dangerous to them both" (208). As if reflecting the boys' disillusionment, the theater itself closes down following their attendance, signifying just one more step in the dehumanization of American life following the Second World War. For what better symbol to depict a loss of innocence than the advent of tiny black and white televisions that people watch in private, reducing not only the power of dreams, but also the sense of community dreams may, at best, provide?

Of all the citizens of Thalia, Billy is most directly hurt by the theater's closing. Alone in the world, except for Sonny, who has recently neglected him, Billy becomes a frightening symbol of the utter isolation anyone could be subjected to as long as people neglect their moral obligations to each other. Only the movie theater, where he was literally conceived, has proved reliable in terms of giving him a needed sense of home and belonging. Therefore, expecting him to be able to distinguish fantasy from reality seems pointless, even though such a distinction would be critical for his survival. Despite Sonny's efforts to persuade him that the theater will never reopen, Billy waits night after night in front of it, believing that it will. The fact that Billy dies while wearing Sonny's eye patches is significant, for they are products of Sonny's silly fight with Duane over Jacy. As such, they symbolically suggest not only Billy's inability to see reality but, in addition, the moral blindness and betrayal the selfish girl helped create. Ultimately, Billy's death thus represents, like Mr. Cecil's unjust firing and Joe Bob's public humiliation, yet another variation on the destructive power of the collective mind in relation to an individual, this time when it completely fails to address a handicapped person's special needs out of ignorance and selfishness.

But McMurtry has included in *The Last Picture Show* an antidote to moral isolation through Ruth Popper's example. It is, therefore, natural that the novel's last scene, inspiring in its implications, takes place between her and Sonny. Above all, it suggests the power of love to enable wounded individuals to confront the painful reality of their lives and, thus, to obtain the possibility of reforming them into something better. Following Billy's death, Sonny attempts to flee town but finds himself too spiritually lost to go through with it. Here, McMurtry appropriately echoes the novel's opening and the loneliness Sonny felt before he met Ruth. "He had the feeling again, the feeling that he was the only person in town" (217). Terrified by the return of such feelings, Sonny instinctively drives to Ruth's house. Despite feelings of guilt, he is now willing to take whatever she dishes out, for only through facing up to her and his social demons can he once and for all avoid the terror of social isolation. Unlike Sam the Lion, who negatively punished Sonny by driving him away for his inhumanity to Billy, Ruth rises to the occasion, allowing channels of communication to remain open while directly expressing her hurt and anger. Sonny, in turn, finds the honest anger behind her accusations of betraying and abandoning her and Billy a relief, for it grounds him and dispels the fear, which he had felt only moments before, of being "blown around for days like a broomweed in the wind" (217). Reaching out his hand, Sonny takes hers in his own and with such a simple, nonverbal gesture signals himself willing—at least for the moment—to take responsibility for a relationship.

This courage on his part is immediately topped by Ruth's own poignant struggle to decide whether or not to take him back. She decides she can forgive him — after all, he is just a boy — but what about the harder question: Can she afford to return his love and risk opening herself up to more inevitable pain and loss? In the end, in true McMurtry fashion, her body, as much as her brave spirit, contains the answer. Taking Sonny's hand and pressing it to her face, Ruth is about to say something "wise or brave or beautiful," but her words are lost because of "the rush of her blood. The quick pulse inside her was all she could feel. . . " (219, 220).

The Last Picture Show, initially published in 1966, was McMurtry's first attempt to create a whole society which he could imaginatively reenter and evaluate in the tradition of Victorian novelists. Like George Eliot in *Middlemarch* and Thomas Hardy in *The Woodlanders,* McMurtry focused on the lives of the small-town individuals with whom he grew up, dramatizing in the process the tragic effects of their personal choices on others. Despite his unsparing portrait of Archer City, including its boredom, isolation, empty sex, materialism, inadequate role models, and above all, suffocation by fundamentalist religion, McMurtry found grounds for hope in the stubborn resiliency of the human spirit and its capacity for love. This is in spite of the fact that his novel came out in a decade when the postmodern alienation of men from each other seemed nearly complete, beyond redemption. *The Last Picture Show* was a major step forward for the young McMurtry, for it paved the way not only for the increasingly sociological concerns of his mature fiction, but for his richest novel to date, *Lonesome Dove.* In it, he would again recreate society in miniature, but this time during the Victorian era itself, when American civilization was finally completing its dominance over the frontier. In the interval, however, McMurtry would produce six new novels with various social milieus, each of which reflects his ongoing fascination with the moral relation of the individual to society.

One such novel, *Terms of Endearment,* opens with a tribute to the first sentence of Jane Austen's *Pride and Prejudice:* "It is a truth universally acknowledged that a single man in possession of a good fortune must be in want of a wife" (1). This ironic line reflects the bias of a mother overly ambitious for her daughters, an appropriate allusion to introduce McMurtry's comic/tragic novel about a mother/daughter relationship marred by the mother's solipsistic ambition. For McMurtry's mother, Aurora, is both proud and prejudiced, as indicated by her opening declaration to her daughter that "the success of a marriage invariably depends on the woman" (3). (In the author's autobiographical *Some Can Whistle,* discussed in Chapter 5, Danny Deck, alias McMurtry, states that he was trying to start a novel with "A broad generality. Think of *Pride and Prejudice . . ."* [49].)

Despite Aurora's selfish eccentricities, she is life affirming, as evidenced by the scolding she gives one of her many suitors, a Dickensian misfit named Vernon. Aurora's speech echoes Ruth's words regarding the hazards of social isolation:

> The point of my criticism was that you've lived fifty years and made no effort to meet anybody, that I can see. You're a perfectly nice, competent, efficient, friendly man, and you might have made some woman very happy, yet you've made no effort to use yourself at all. You've made no one really happy, not even yourself, and now you're so set in your ridiculous ways that you wouldn't know how to begin to relate to another person. It's shameful really. You're a wasted resource. (208)

During the first part of the novel, one filled with an odd assortment of characters with contrasting styles and manners, Aurora (a former New Englander transplanted to Texas) learns to cope with middle-aged widowhood and the mortality implied by her daughter Emma's making her a grandmother. She ultimately does this by adopting a lover whom she uses to bring together the eclectic collection of suitors she has entertained during the course of the story. At her section's close, she experiences a reassuring moment which transcends time by connecting her youthful past to the present. And gazing out her bedroom window she watches approvingly as her new lover, the General, greets her other boyfriends as host for the first time:

> Alberto, she could see, had his arms full of flowers. When he saw Vernon beside him and the General at the door, he looked puzzled. His instinct was to bristle, and yet he was not quite certain if he should bristle just then. Vernon had put on a Stetson hat for the occasion. Aurora waited, smiling, and then by peeking over, saw the General step out on the porch and extend his hand. (322)

But McMurtry does not conclude his book on such a light note, for the title of the novel itself suggests the human limitations of relationships as antidotes for isolation and death. In the second section, Aurora's daughter is abruptly discovered to have cancer, as a result of which Emma "for the first time in her life . . . felt beyond the efficacy of love" (358). And in perhaps the novel's most poignant line, Emma realizes, much like a disenchanted Hardy heroine,[10] that the man whose looks she had once fallen for now appears a virtual stranger. As she studies her unfaithful husband's aging face, she cannot even recall "what the terms of endearment had been, or how they had been lost for so long" (361). Nevertheless, before she dies, Emma displays the strength of her down-to-earth simplicity, which enables her to be more in touch with the moral reality of one's obligations to others than either her flighty, egoistic mother or her irresponsible husband. An example of this would be her wise reminder to Flap regarding the future care of her children: "We're thinking of them. . . . We're not thinking of the way we'd like to think of ourselves" (361).

Another example of a McMurtry novel written in the interval before *Lonesome Dove* which treats comically the theme of the relation of the individual to society is *Cadillac Jack*. Thirty-three years old and twice divorced, Jack, the main character, is a modern drifter and a study in the pros and cons of social freedom and isolation versus commitment and responsibility. As Jean Arbor, the voice of moral stability in the novel, says to him at one point, being committed to another person means "holding still and being bored half the time" (386). At another point, she comments, "It's very interesting that you're never quite free of kids" (375). Despite such sentiments, when Jack wakes up in Jean's sunny bedroom with her kids tumbling on the bed, he is forced to confront the life he has sacrificed due to his compulsive traveling as a dealer in antiques:

> Still, if I had been a big disappointment, she seemed to be weathering it nicely. She looked quite happy, sitting on the bed with the girls. They formed a bright ensemble in their red bathrobes. Belinda sat across my feet, so that it was not easy for me to sit up and drink my coffee. There was a nice smell in the bed, namely the smell of young females and one woman, mixing with the smell of hot coffee. (373)

As a former Texas rodeo performer in the midst of an identity crisis, Jack also enables McMurtry to cast a sharp sociological eye on the government workers and social climbers in the city of Washington, where the story is set. Their mostly despair-ridden lives reflect a lack of spirit in a city which perversely values form over substance, a fact humorously underscored when Jack is asked to arrange an exhibit of boots from his native state which attracts the city's "A" crowd. In such an environment, even a casual lunch at the Department of Transportation can become a memorable lesson in dehumanization:

> The workers — I guess they should be called bureaucrats — poured off the food line carrying hamburgers on styrofoam plates. Then they grabbed a styrofoam cup, scooped up a few ice cubes, and moved past a row of spigots that dispersed liquids on the order of iced tea and Pepsi-Cola.
> I don't eat in cafeterias much — just being in the middle of such a vast one

was a little daunting. The people shuffling along in the food line didn't have the anticipatory look people usually have when they're waiting to be fed. Most people assume that if they're going to be fed the food will probably taste good, but nowhere in the cafeteria did I see a face lit with the prospect of eating something that might taste good. Instead of looking like people who were about to eat they looked like people who had lined up to get polio shots, or something. (220)

Jack's other Washington girlfriend, Cindy, is a beautiful but superficial social climber from Santa Barbara who views him as an amusing detour on her road to the top. Preparing to escort her to an important party, Jack finds himself unable to forget their lovemaking only moments before. As a result, Cindy proceeds to lecture him on the extreme decorum which life in the nation's capitol demands:

"Oblivia doesn't understand people who don't do things at the right time," she said. "She was brought up among successful people."

"Come on," I said. "Nobody does everything at the right time."

"Oh yeah, around here they do," Cindy said. "Somebody like the Secretary of State isn't going to get a hard-on just before a party."

It was plain that my aberrant behavior intrigued Cindy a little. It might make me unfit for a Cabinet post, but I had a feeling it kept me in the running with Harris, for at least one more day.

"I just don't know what she'll think of you," she said, laying down her brush. The uncertainty seemed to excite her. I was an ambiguous factor, socially and otherwise. On that provocative note, we left for the party." (136)

Larry McMurtry's attempt to come to terms with his personal alienation through his art would continue as his career progressed and took him far from his rural origins. From the vantage point of success, the author would leave fundamentalist religion and Archer City behind but continue to explore provocative questions regarding human relationships. Among these would be the inadequacy of the human ego in isolation, its frequent desire for fantasy over reality, for selfishness over humanity, and above all, how death inevitably brings to the foreground the need for strength and love on a personal basis in a modern world missing shared transcendental values. As McMurtry's early college letters forecast, his ambivalent attitude toward the urban world of culture which increasingly embraced him would be just as real as his ambivalence to the world he left behind. His growing preoccupation with this conflict and his attempts to come to terms with it would first come to a dramatic head in his autobiographical novel, *All My Friends Are Going to Be Strangers*.

CHAPTER THREE

Lonesome Dove

THE CONFLICT BETWEEN CIVILIZATION AND NATURE

> "You have been well educated, well tended, and you have be-
> come the wife of a professional man of unusually good family.
> Surely you ought to make the best of your position."
> "I don't see that I ought. I wish I had never got into it. I
> wish you had never, never thought of educating me. I wish I
> worked in the woods like Marty South! I hate genteel life,
> and I want to be no better than she!"
> "Why?" said her amazed father.
> "Because cultivation has only brought me inconveniences
> and troubles. I say again, I wish you had never sent me to
> those fashionable schools you set your mind on. It all arose
> out of that, father. . . ."
> — Thomas Hardy, *The Woodlanders*

THE CLOSE of Larry McMurtry's fifth novel finds his most clearly autobiographical character, Danny Deck, stranded in the flowing waters of the Rio
Grande, unable to reconcile his simple rural past with the confusing world
of urban culture of which he has suddenly become a part. His spiritual
crisis would reflect the author's own as he achieved worldly success.
McMurtry's repeated attempts to resolve his sense of dislocation would
find their most rewarding results with the publication of *Lonesome Dove*.

But it would take a number of years after his portrayal of Danny's struggle for McMurtry to achieve the equilibrium and emotional distance from his Texas home which were needed. Earlier, his ambivalence had been largely directed at his rural past, infusing his portraits of his native state with realistic tensions which made them instantly memorable. But now that he had attained sudden literary and movie success, his diffidence grew to encompass the glamorous new worlds of publishing and Hollywood opening to him. Like Thomas Hardy, McMurtry would remain an eccentric outsider even as he moved in special circles of the elite and sophisticated. And like Hardy's character Grace, whose words open this chapter, his heart and spirit would soon partly long to return to his earlier home associated with nature. But before he could, he would leave Texas and bravely explore new settings for his novels.

McMurtry's personal journey from a rural to an urban setting, and his resulting anxiety, mirrors the Victorian Age's sudden movement from a rural to an urban economy. Kathleen Tillotson has referred to "the drag of the past and the pull of the present" (Gilmour 57) which Victorian novelists felt in response to radical social change. At the center of *All My Friends Are Going to Be Strangers* is Danny, who suffers similar feelings as a result of the sudden publication of his first novel and the subsequent move to California from his home state of Texas.

Of McMurtry critics to date, Raymond L. Neinstein has proven most effective in pointing out the ironic relationship between Danny's alienation and his use of language. As Neinstein states of Danny in his afterward to the novel:

> As a character in a novel, and a novelist himself, and the narrator of the story of his own displacement and growing distrust of language as the mediating term that both connects us to and at the same time inevitably distances us from the world, creating the sense of exile from a place we have never "really" known but for which we have always been nostalgic, what can Danny do but vanish? (293)

Realizing in despair the limitations of language as a means of simultaneously connecting him to his present world and a world of the past he has never known firsthand, Danny attempts to destroy his newly completed novel by drowning it in a river. Appropriately, as he does so, literary references flood his mind (Jack London, O. Henry, Ambrose Bierce, Thomas Mann, Homer) juxtaposed with the people he has loved in person but from whom he has become increasingly distant. Before wading into the Rio Grande, Danny stares at his own manuscript with contempt, poignantly realizing that "the black marks on paper" lacked "faces . . . Jill had a face. Emma had a face. My words didn't" (278). And in a moment of self-discovery, he understands that as a successful writer, he has sacrificed the ordinary simplicity of a life spent close to nature's rhythms, a life represented by "the door to Emma's kitchen or to all such places" (281). Instead, he has set himself on a course of compromises between his art and his need for others, between civilization and nature, a life among those misfits denied completeness, such as "Exiled ping-pong players and the old ladies with dogs on their arms" and "Godwin and Jenny and all those who had missed the same door" (281). To live such a life as an artist requires self-acceptance and courage, qualities which Danny, despite his mysterious disappearance, must have ultimately found, for he reemerges as a successful television writer in *Some Can Whistle*.

But before McMurtry would again bring his alter ego to life, he would return to writing about Texas on a grander scale than ever before. For he had learned through experience that his ambivalence to Archer City and his heritage, like his later ambivalence with success, was largely an internal conflict requiring management and attempts at reconciliation, rather than estrangement from its external sources. The author's maturity and self-awareness would be reflected in the balanced treatment he gave his major themes of the relation of the individual to society and the conflict between civilization and nature in *Lonesome Dove*.

The novel's opening quote by T. K. Whipple underscores McMurtry's grand intention of objectifying his personal ambivalence to include all America: "All America lies at the end of the wilderness road, and our past is not a dead past, but still lives in us. Our forefathers had civilization inside themselves, the wild outside. We live in the civilization they created, but within us the wildness still lingers. What they dreamed, we live, and what they lived, we dream" (9). In *The Last Picture Show*, McMurtry showed how modern civilization contains the seeds of its own destruction. T. K. Whipple's words illustrate how in *Lonesome Dove* McMurtry intended to go a step further and, like many Victorian novelists, confront head on the immediate past he had always dreamed of and tended to idealize. In the process, he would release new energies as he recreated in haunting detail a simpler world linked to nature on the verge of extinction.

The novel's opening would brilliantly set up the novel's major theme, the inevitable triumph of civilization and its comforts over the dangers posed by the frontier: "When Augustus came out on the porch the blue pigs were eating a rattlesnake — not a very big one. It had probably been crawling around looking for shade when it ran into pigs. They were having a fine tug-of-war with it, and its rattling days were over. The sow had it by the neck, and the shoat had the tail" (13). The blue pigs belonging to Gus are symbols of civilization while the rattlesnake — its rattling days gone — symbolizes the former potential dangers lurking in the Eden-like garden of nature. The fact that the female pig is the one with the snake by the neck suggests the importance of women in civilizing the frontier. Moreover, the fact that McMurtry chooses an image of civilization literally devouring nature underscores the central irony Whipple's words introduced: Once nature's external dangers are brought under control, they are immediately replaced by more elusive internal ones. Thus, by succeeding in taming outward nature, those responsible for it are doomed to a kind of failure.

Gus's pigs are small but important symbols of the aristocratic background he abandoned when he left Tennessee[1], and as his sign later makes clear, they are personal items not to be shared or rented. Appropriately, they follow him on the cattle drive, and when he is on his deathbed refusing to have his second leg amputated, he says in justification that he might "want to kick a pig" (781). Clearly, Gus's cherished pigs are playful manifestations of his need to challenge civilization, a need for which he would rather die than be unable to insure. Sadly, following his death, they end up being killed for food (813).

If Augustus embodies McMurtry's ambivalent relationship with civilization, Call embodies the author's ambivalent relationship with nature. As the narrator informs the reader in the first chapter, while Call tries immediately to dominate and kill snakes, Augustus first tries to accommodate them (14). Call's inclination to dominate nature insures survival on the frontier while Augustus's gift for peaceful accommodations keeps civilization humming. It is little wonder that Gus is the reluctant one when Jake proposes abandoning the relative civility and safety of Lonesome Dove. Neither is it surprising that the progression from nature to civilization, from rigidity to flexibility, is mirrored in the first syllable of Call's first name, "Wood," followed eventually by "Crae," the last syllable of Gus's name, suggesting "ray of light" or knowledge.

Nowhere is Augustus's close link with civilization more apparent than in his constant use of words. As the narrator tells the reader, "Augustus was notorious all over Texas for the sound of his voice" (26). And nowhere is McMurtry's ambivalence to language more strongly felt than in his description of the formation of Gus's sign, a sign meant to establish the Hat Creek Outfit's identity for outsiders. Recalling the difficult Latin Jude associates with Christmaster in *Jude the Obscure,* the sign in *Lonesome Dove* becomes a similarly profound symbol embodying the hope and alienation brought about by civilization.[2] The sign writing is left to Augustus, and in the process it becomes an illustration not only of his personal vanity, but of the corrupting vanity associated with culture in general. No mere collection of names, the completed sign states what the outfit will or will not sell or rent, and even concludes with an intriguing phrase in Latin. The sign's additions show how the vanity of civilization serves to alienate. Even unassuming Deets falls under its spell when his friend Pea gets his name on it.

> Deets had ridden with [Call] for years, through all weathers and all dangers, over country so barren they had more than once had to kill a horse to have meat, and in all those years Deets had given cheerful service. Then, all because of the sign, he went into a sulk and stayed in it until Augustus finally spotted him looking wistfully at it one day and figured it out. When Augustus told Call of his condition, Call was further outraged. "That damn sign's ruint this outfit," he said, and went into a sulk himself. He had known Augustus was vain but would never have suspected Deets or Pea of such a failing. (87)

The ultimate irony in all this is that Augustus's final addition to the sign is a Latin motto—"Uva uvam vivendo varia fit"—which he takes from his father's schoolbook not because he knows what it means, but because it looks good (89). Appropriately, the Latin phrase has produced varying translations, but one put forth by Ernestine Sewell—"The cluster of grapes—many-sided, parti-colored, diverse—through living, beget one grape" (224)—is particularly suggestive of McMurtry's ambivalence regarding language and civilization.[3] Language and civilization do, indeed, unify, seemingly making mankind one, but beneath comforting appearances lie various individual interpretations determined by individual needs. Augustus's Latin phrase is a perfect symbol of this, not only because Latin is associated with the origins of Western civilization, but precisely because it is sufficiently incomprehensible to allow various readings and/or misreadings. As Augustus explains to Call "a sign's a kind of tease. . . . It ought to make a man stop and consider what he wants out of life in the next few days" (89). His words rightly imply that the sign's effectiveness comes from its being simultaneously reductive and suggestive.

McMurtry's ambivalence to language and civilization, symbolized by Gus's sign, helps define the identities of the novel's major characters. For through their contrasting relationships with language, the futures of Call, Newt, Clara, and Lorena are largely determined.

In contrast to Augustus's love of language as an instrument of socializing and making people hold up a mirror to themselves, Call prefers the more basic language of nature to that of men. Early on, the reader learns that Call liked to "listen to the country" (26), get away from the other men, and "sniff the breeze and let the country talk" (26). He misses the dangers of the untamed wilderness, a time when "a man who presumed to stake out a Comanche would do well to keep his rifle cocked" (28). For him, language is unimportant and potentially distorting, for it appears to have nothing to do with a man's true essence or ability to work closely with nature, feelings reflected in his inability to recall Pea Eye's real name, a man who has given him three decades of loyal service (87). Call's need for danger and action over civilized talk and self-reflection lead to his tragic decision to stake out a new territory in Montana.

Facing manhood poised between the opposing worlds of Call and Gus, Newt's confused relationship with language underscores an orphan's longing for a clear identity. As Call's illegitimate and unacknowledged son, his search for a true last name poses the provocative question of whether or not finding his name and becoming formally civilized will benefit him versus (as Call believes) his being better off by remaining part of the frontier. At the start of the novel, Newt knows only the latter world, for he believes that free-spirited Jake Spoon is his father, and in his dreams Call takes him "to the high plains he had heard about but never seen. There was never anyone else in the dreams: just him and the Captain, on horseback in a beautiful country" (34). In this context, Gus's constructing the sign foreshadows Newt's ultimate claiming by civilization and his corresponding disillusionment, a fate his youth protects him from: "Newt recognized that he was rightly too young to have his name on the sign and never suggested the possibility to anyone, though it would have pleased him mightily if someone suggested it for him. No one did, but then Deets had to wait nearly two years before his name appeared on the sign, and Newt resigned himself to waiting too" (87). Ironically, Newt's claiming by civilization occurs largely by default, for Call never openly acknowledges his son, despite Gus's protests.

Although Clara, Augustus's great love, has no interest in his sign, her relation to language is an important indication of her role in the novel. Of all the major characters, hers is most closely associated with the domestication of language and the frontier. Recalling Dorothea in *Middlemarch* and other Victorian heroines who yearn for sophistication and culture, McMurtry treats sympathetically Clara's desire for a world of learning denied her as a nineteenth-century woman. Furthermore, McMurtry uses her to make a strong statement of the conflict between art and reality. Reading novels by authors like George Eliot who describe a level of civilization foreign to her own, Clara dreams of being a novelist herself until her boys die.

> Once the sight of the writing tablets had made her hopeful, but after those deaths it ceased to matter. . . . She burned the tablets one day, trembling with anger and pain, as if paper and not the weather had been somehow responsible for the deaths of her boys. And, for a time, she stopped reading magazines. The stories in them seemed hateful to her: How could people talk that way and spend their time going to balls and parties, when children died and had to be buried?
>
> But a few years passed, and Clara went back to the stories in the magazines. . . . Bob didn't like it, but he tolerated it. No other woman read as much as his wife. (591)

Just as Call is unconsciously threatened by the verbal gymnastics of Gus's sign, so Clara's pragmatic husband distrusts his wife's act of reading, which he associates with vanity.

The ending of the novel highlights McMurtry's use of language as a symbol of his ambivalence to civilization. When Call cannot tell Newt that he is his father, when all he can do is produce inarticulate sounds from his throat, he shows his inability to accept civilization (822). As Call tells Clara, he considers his horse — part of nature — more valuable than his name (831). Furthermore, the two letters Gus writes his women before he dies (which Call is forced to deliver) underscore the triumph of civilization from which his own death saves him. Though Clara has finally prompted Gus into the civilized role of letter writer, his death insures that she will never have him in a domestic context. Instead, Call will bear his friend's body to Texas. And by not allowing Clara to read Gus's letter to her, Lorena instinctively refuses to allow Gus's assimilation into the civilized world even after his death (829).

Unlike Clara, Lorena distrusts the refinements of civilization, which have kept her an outsider even as she is attracted to them. After passing up the opportunity to hear Gus's letter, she stands over his coffin and thinks: "They'll all forget you — they got their doings. . . . But I won't Gus. Whenever it comes morning or night, I'll think of you. You came and got me away from him. She can forget and they can forget, but I won't, never, Gus" (830). Her thoughts closely echo the words of Marty South at the end of Thomas Hardy's *The Woodlanders*:

> "Now, my own, own love," she whispered, "You are mine, and only mine; for she has forgot 'ee at last, although for her you died! But I — whenever I get up I'll think of 'ee, and whenever I lie down I'll think of 'ee again. When-

ever I plant as you planted; and whenever I split a gad, and whenever I turn
the cider wring, I'll say none could do it like you. If ever I could forget your
name let me forget home and heaven! . . . But no, no, my love, I never can
forget 'ee: for you was a good man, and did good things!" (444)

Notice the emphasis on morning and night, in that order, to convey the
idea of constant thought of the deceased in both passages. In addition,
Lorena rejects Clara's world for that of Gus, who bravely rescued her from
the Indian Blue Duck, while Marty rejects the self-centered but cultivated
Grace for the poor woodsman Giles, who dies taking care of another. The
parallels suggest that McMurtry, in writing *Lonesome Dove,* was partly inspired by Marty's eloquent rejection of civilization in favor of the honest
people who live close to nature.

Finally, the fate of Gus's sign at the novel's end underscores Call's unwillingness to gracefully accept the inevitable triumph of civilization.
When Call uses the sign as Gus's gravestone, all that remains on it in terms
of language is what he himself would have put there: "Hat Creek Cattle
Company and Livery Emporium." Just as Danny Deck's literary manuscript was destroyed by water at the end of *All My Friends Are Going to Be
Strangers,* so Augustus's sign has been crudely stripped in his absence of its
imaginative and literary aspects, which are simultaneously inspirational
and reductive. And without the individual names which encourage ego-
based conflicts between men, Call ironically cannot provide a record of his
oldest, closest friend. This point is driven home when a young couple ar-
rives on the scene in a wagon. Their understandable confusion over the
sign prompts Call to scratch on it his friend's initials — A. M. — which, in
relation to time, ironically suggest the beginning of a new day in contrast
to the old era which Call wants remembered:

> The business of the sign worried him, one more evidence of Augustus's abil-
> ity to vex well beyond the grave. If one young man supposed there was a
> livery stable nearby, others would do the same. People might be inconve-
> nienced for days, wandering through the limestone hills, trying to find a
> company who were mostly ghosts.
>
> Besides, Augustus's name wasn't on the sign, though it was his grave. No
> one might even realize it *was* his grave. Call walked back up the hill and got
> out his knife, thinking he might carve the name on the other side of the
> board, but the old board was so dry and splintery he felt he might destroy it
> altogether if he worked on it much. Finally he just scratched A.M. on the
> other side of the board. It wasn't much, and it wouldn't last, he knew. Some-
> body would just get irritated at not finding the livery stable and bust the sign
> up. (840–41)

McMurtry's skillful treatment of the conflict between civilization and nature in *Lonesome Dove* is closely related to his interest in the relation of the individual to society which formed the previous chapter's focus. His criticism of civilized society involves portraying it as a collection of conflicting egos similar to William Makepeace Thackeray's depiction in *Vanity Fair*. Yet at the same time, McMurtry echoes George Eliot in his concentration on the individual ego seeking strength through others in a world lacking spiritual values. Just as McMurtry's ambivalence to civilization is reflected in Gus's paradoxical sign, which adds structural symmetry by appearing at the opening and close of the novel in its states of formation and deterioration, so his ambivalence to society is reflected in Bolivar's ringing of the dinner bell, which frames the story.

When Call encounters Bol loudly ringing the dinner bell as he returns to Lonesome Dove, few are around to hear it. Once the loud ringing of the bell signaling dinner was a source of constant annoyance to Call and Augustus, though it ironically signaled the most social gathering of the day following work, a civilized ritual which replaced private communion with nature or beauty. Upon Call's return, the bell takes on a bittersweet quality as it suggests the permanent absence of old friends such as Jake and Gus, people who made dinner with their talk something special. As the narrator states:

> He [Call] rode into Lonesome Dove late on a day in August, only to be startled by the harsh clanging of the dinner bell, the one Bolivar had loved to beat with the broken crowbar. The sound made him feel that he rode through a land of ghosts. He felt lost in his mind and wondered if all the boys would be there when he got home.
>
> But when he trotted through the chaparral toward the Hat Creek barn, he saw it was old Bolivar himself, beating the same bell with the same piece of crowbar. The old man's hair was white and his serape filthier than ever.
>
> When Bolivar looked up and saw the Captain riding out of the sunset, he dropped the piece of crowbar, narrowly missing his foot. His return to Mexico had been a trial and disappointment. (841)

The ending of *Lonesome Dove* parallels the ending of *The Last Picture Show* in their common focus on individuals attempting to reaffirm their identities through connecting with other individuals associated with a particular place. In the case of Bolivar, the individual being reconnected with has specific links to society and culture. This is seen by his Mexican heritage combined with his white hair, which recall Sonny's encounter with the white-haired Mexican who resembled Sam the Lion (a symbol of community and culture in the earlier novel).

Other important parallels between the two endings are worth mentioning. Call's words of reassurance to Bol — "It's alright" — (842) are remarkably similar to Ruth's words — "Never you mind" — to Sonny (220). It is both moving and ironic that the stoic, self-reliant Call should finally offer up words of reassurance to another highly independent man, a man who once rang the dinner bell "not because he wanted anybody to come and eat" but because he "liked the sound"; a man who, despite protests to the contrary, refused "to take orders"; a man who vacillated ambivalently back and forth to Mexico where his wife and daughters resided; a man whose "sense of independence was undiminished" (25). After comforting Bol, Call discovers the Dry Bean saloon has burned down in his absence. A main source of communal cultural experience with its piano and Lorena, its loss serves a similar role symbolically as the closing down of the picture show at the end of the earlier novel. For, despite McMurtry's conflicting feelings with regard to culture, both works end in affirmation of its extreme importance through suggesting the devastating impact its disappearance has on those left behind. (Xavier Wanz, the novel's most refined character, suggests Billy at the conclusion of *The Last Picture Show* in that he cannot survive Lorena's departure and dies as a result.)

Lonesome Dove's emphasis on love, friendship, and society as possible sources of salvation is highly Victorian. J. Hillis Miller has written that Victorian fiction "may be said to have as its fundamental theme an exploration of the various ways in which a man may seek to make a god of another person in a world without God, or at any rate in a world where the traditional ways in which the self may be related to God no longer seem open (*The Form of Victorian Fiction* 96). He has stated further that "often this search for a valid foundation for the self is dramatized in a woman rather than a man" (96). Relevant in this regard is Ernestine Sewell's suggestion that Lorena is the "soiled dove" most closely linked to the book's title (221). Through her, the lonely individual search for transcendence is most obviously manifested. The image of a dove implies the innocent purity and beauty of such a goal — even for such a supposedly soiled outcast as Lorena.

This frustrating search for God or fulfillment through relationship with another so reminiscent of George Eliot or Thomas Hardy is repeated over and over in *Lonesome Dove* on a scale dwarfing McMurtry's portrayal of the same phenomenon in *The Last Picture Show*. The author originally claimed that·he thought Gus's Latin phrase at the bottom of his sign meant "the grape changes its hue [ripens] by looking at another grape."[4] This is suggestive, for not only does Lorena seek such fulfillment first through Jake and then Augustus, but her lonely struggle becomes mirrored in the way most men of the Hat Creek Outfit, particularly Dish, seek fulfillment through her. Furthermore, it is reflected in Newt's desire to find fulfillment not only through Lorena, but through Call and Jake. And it is seen in July Johnson's hopeless idealization of his wife Elmire, as well as Xavier Wanz's fatal idealization of Lorena. Perhaps most of all, it is shown in Call's very real, though never acknowledged, dependence on Gus for a sense of purpose and identity, a dependence which complicates and ultimately thwarts Augustus's and Clara's latent desire over a period of many years to find fulfillment through each other. Miller describes the Victorian novel as "a structure of interpenetrating minds . . . the minds of the characters as they behold or know one another" (*The Form of Victorian Fiction* 2). What could be a more accurate description of *Lonesome Dove* as it takes characters like Call, Gus, Clara, and Lorena and fills them with the consciousness of others (living and dead) as they attempt to find the secret of transcendence?

The chaotic mismatches between such characters seeking love and fulfillment are given heightened urgency by the constant hazards of nature which they face with Hardy-like regularity. As they move away from the civilization represented by Lonesome Dove, nature becomes an increasingly deadly presence. At least one critic has complained of McMurtry's rather fanciful portrayal of nature's laws (Abernethy 1). But to do so is to miss the point, for through the artful use of such fantastic mishaps the author imaginatively underscores his message of the individual's tenuous emotional state and his or her dependence on others.

Thus, to fully appreciate the complex symbolic underpinnings of McMurtry's novel, it is necessary to examine not only his portrayal of outward nature, but inner human nature and their mutual need to be tamed by civilization. In "McMurtry's Cowboy-God in *Lonesome Dove,*" Ernestine Sewell finds a Freudian composite in the novel consisting of Call as "Superego; Gus, Ego; and Jake, Id." She asserts, "When Jake the Id dies, nothing seems to go right anymore. When Gus's tempering Ego is gone, Call becomes a confused old man" (224). While one normally associates the super-ego with civilization, Sewell's analogy is helpful in that Call's relation to nature depends on his need to dominate it, thereby reflecting the author's fear of repression and its consequences. Furthermore, Gus is associated with the positive trait of accommodation the author links with civilization and which he, for the most part, found lacking in his own ancestors. Finally, in Jake, the author represents the very real dangers of both inner and outer nature without controls.

Therefore, when Jake rides into Lonesome Dove near the beginning of the story, he unwittingly sets in motion the final symbolic deterioration of the frontier way of life. The futility of Call's watch by the river reveals a hard won state of equilibrium between man and nature, an equilibrium underscored by the two words which make up the outfit's name: "hat" and "creek." The name implies the fragile balance between civilization (symbolized by "hat," a protective covering for the part of men's heads which contains their minds) and nature (symbolized by "creek," a more manageable form of the river in *All My Friends Are Going to Be Strangers* linked with nature and the chaotic, potentially deadly, life force). This balance, which the relatively educated Augustus has grown accustomed to, is permanently upset when Call takes Jake's bait concerning the opportunities offered by the untamed Montana wilderness. Using Sewell's framework, Call (the superego who tames nature by repressing it) gives into temptation and ignores Gus (the ego who attempts a civilized balance between man and nature) and listens instead to the unstable Jake (the dangerous id who exemplifies nature's wildness and who, uncontrolled, disrupts civilization). Like the soul of a dysfunctional human being, the soul of the novel represented by Gus becomes ultimately doomed, for he alone seeks a civilized balance between man and nature and is the individual most stable in his relations with others.

The cattle drive which follows outwardly dramatizes the cost of Call's tragic mistake. The multiple deaths which eventually distinguish it merit careful examination. Appropriately, the drive's first tragedy involves a river and snakes and the death of a character highly dependent upon civilization. Sean, newly arrived from Ireland, is a sensitive boy who sings and cries for his mother and the beautiful green homeland left behind. Though experiencing extreme culture shock, Sean represents man's universal dependence on civilization, a fact underscored by the common heritage he shares with his seeming opposite, Woodrow Call. For as Gus reminds Call earlier in the novel, he is technically not an American having been born in Scotland many years before (25). The way Sean meets his death is also symbolic. The snakes which bite poor Sean recall the snake in the novel's opening paragraph associated with the danger lurking in Eden's garden. And just as the snakes are linked with nature's deadly wildness, so is the river. In a dinner exchange in the opening chapter, Call angrily tells Gus, "I wish they'd [the whores] drownt you then." Undaunted, Augustus replies, "Drown me? Why, if anybody had tried it, those girls would have clawed them to shreds" (24). Symbolically, Gus asserts that women — associated with civilization — will save him from nature, a fate he later in the novel ironically avoids. So in the contest between civilization and nature, Sean's death by snakes while crossing a river on a horse suggests the last triumph of nature over civilization before the end of the frontier era when cowboys freely roamed. For not only does it include the unexpected dethroning of a male from his horse by symbols of nature's wildness, it is the only death on the cattle drive caused by outward nature (the rest involve men's inner nature).

Jake's death, for example, arises from a failure in personal morality, a failure which throws into question the morality of that code of justice which Rangers, such as Jake, Augustus, and Call, fought to uphold. Just as earlier McMurtry exposed the reductive quality of language using Gus's sign, so here he demonstrates the primitive quality of frontier justice and the kind of men who enforce it without consideration for extenuating circumstances. Though Gus and Call love Jake like a brother, they have done little to inhibit his selfish, amoral impulses, which inevitably lead him to casually fall in with a group of thieves and murderers when it suits his purpose. Thus, by carrying out the rigid letter of frontier justice against their friend by hanging him, Call and Gus cannot avoid exposing the limitations inherent in the simplistic idealism they have lived for.

Both Deets's and Augustus's deaths naturally follow. Appropriately, Deets's death is the result of a gentle, almost motherly impulse associated with civilization. Picking up a crying baby without thought of himself, Deets fails to respond to an Indian's lance pointed at him, a lance Call appears too slow to intercept, as if uncharacteristically caught off guard. Call's miscalculation mirrors Gus's own when he foolishly rides into a herd of Indians alone (even though Pea Eye is nearby) in a brash last surge of vitality which leads him to receive a fatal arrow.

If Augustus dies from his fear of being dependent on civilization combined with his vanity, Call dies in spirit from his stoicism and the emptiness resulting from an isolated life spent close to nature. As already suggested, he cannot bring himself—despite Gus's and Clara's protests—to acknowledge the flexible quality of humanity associated with civilization by admitting his past mistakes and openly giving his son, Newt, his name. Nonetheless, there are indications of mellowing as his world crumbles. For example, his reluctantly agreeing to carry out Gus's wish to be buried in Clara's orchard is, in a sense, completely out of character, for it means carrying out a purely sentimental gesture which openly acknowledges his close attachment to another human being. Furthermore, when Deets dies, Call creates an eloquent sign to serve as his tombstone.[5] By the end of the novel, it is impossible to imagine Call ever entirely returning to his former self because he no longer has full confidence in the cowboy dream which has determined the shape of his life. (As if in confirmation of his fate, Call receives a bullet wound from an Indian on the last part of his journey back to Lonesome Dove.) Instead, he will be faced with a civilized world of increasing domestication and women's influence, a world he has little desire or ability to adjust to.[6]

In contrast to Call's stoicism and fear of women, Gus's gift for accommodation and ability to connect with others in a positive way makes him a paradigm of the power of demonstrative love. Nowhere is this more evident than in the manner in which he saves Lorena and nurses her back to emotional health following her capture by Blue Duck. Sexually abused and an outcast of genteel society, Lorena nevertheless has retained much of her astonishing beauty and spirit, a spirit which reveals itself in her dream to reside in the civilized city of San Francisco. When kidnapped by Blue Duck as a direct result of Jake's irresponsibility, she is forced to face the direct opposite of her genteel vision. An Indian half-breed bent on forever disrupting the white man's efforts to civilize the wilderness, he is bitterly sadistic with his blatant disregard for the human soul and its search for transcendence. Simultaneously he becomes symbolic of what society, at its best, protects most individuals from and what can happen to the lone ego when it becomes alienated from society and seeks to strike back with id-like irresponsibility. Through him, McMurtry suggests that even worse than the physical hazards of outward nature are the internal hazards of the human mind in isolation gone astray. Even Blue Duck's name conveys a suggestion of nature deformed — ducks are normally not blue. Appropriately, it is the courtly Augustus who rescues Lorena from her experience of rape and torture, which, though physical violations, were, more importantly, emotional ones. He achieves this as a direct result of love and an intuitive understanding of the individual moral support she needs: "He [Gus] didn't talk about what happened to her but treated her as he always had in Lonesome Dove" (468). Like Ruth in *The Last Picture Show,* Gus demonstrates the potential for people through courage, love, and self-awareness to provide genuine sources of meaning to others in society.

Lonesome Dove remains McMurtry's most masterful work to date, a fact deriving in no small part from his extraordinary ability to use his personal alienation to suggest the ambiguities surrounding the conflict between civilization and nature. In the process, he shows not only the virtues of pride, hard work, and community spirit associated with the frontier, but also its harshness, intolerance, and mindless brutality. He manages in addition to suggest the reductive peace associated with modern civilization, its corrupting vanity, its lack of positive role models, but also its humanity, its toleration of personal differences, and a new awareness of the inner needs of the individual for self-affirmation. The author's maturity enables him to present a balanced appraisal and create a most Victorian narrative voice, a neutral voice effortlessly able to penetrate the diverse minds of numerous characters from the recent past, characters who continually attempt to understand themselves and others and achieve accommodation despite the sudden changes they endure. That the novel closes without easy answers, other than the inevitable movement toward civilization and affirmation of the need for reconciliation which Victorian culture and Augustus have both embodied, is part of its strength.[7]

McMurtry's obsessive desire to strike a balance between civilization and nature finds expression in two novels he wrote before and after *Lonesome Dove*: *Somebody's Darling* and *Texasville*. Though neither novel has the scope of *Lonesome Dove*, they both are rich in symbols as they focus on modern civilization in a state of decadence and on highly successful, though jaded, individuals removed from nature and seeking meaning in their lives.

What is a better metaphor for modern civilization than Hollywood? In *The Last Picture Show*, McMurtry showed it providing positive communal cultural experiences in addition to harboring potentially destructive forces via its substitution of fantasy for reality. *Somebody's Darling*, with its Hollywood setting, suggests that the confusion of fantasy with reality can easily and ironically overwhelm those responsible for the creation of popular icons.

In the midst of this artificial world is a would-be survivor named Jill Peel. A cartoonist turned director, she is at once highly cerebral and creative, yet at the same time frustrated sexually. Like Sue Bridehead in Thomas Hardy's *Jude the Obscure*, her conflicted personality arises from her inability to find a relationship both physically and spiritually satisfying.[8] Thinking, therefore, that she must constantly separate the spiritual from the physical, her most promising relationships with men (Danny in *All My Friends Are Going to Be Strangers* and Joe in *Somebody's Darling*) remain, for the most part, platonic.

The tension created by this conflict between civilization and nature, between formal relations and underlying lust, is alluded to by her friend Joe Percy at the start of the novel. Over Sunday brunch with Jill, he boldly suggests a similarity between the way "women handle coffee cups" and the way "men would like women to handle their toys" (13). His analogy defines the "terms of endearment" of a friendship based on the attraction of opposites. For, while he is an aging screenwriter whose womanizing has gotten out of control following his wife's death, Jill is a young woman obsessed with work and possessed with qualities of self-abnegation and seriousness which threaten enjoyment of life. Just as the Sonny/Ruth relationship in *The Last Picture Show* serves as a structural framing device to suggest the transcending power of relationships between individuals in a constricting society, so the Jill Peel/Joe Percy relationship serves as a structural framing device surrounding the selfish fantasies of greed and lust perpetuated by Hollywood's egoistic zoo. Appropriately, the novel is divided into three parts, with the first and last sections told from Joe's and Jill's points of view, respectively. Jill's abusive, manipulative lover Owen dominates the second section, symbolically suggesting the lustful solipsism which could destroy her relationship with Joe. Furthermore, the sexual reference regarding coffee cups mentioned in the opening scene is recalled in the last big scene between her and Joe.

It is an important scene and one of personal growth for Jill because she finally, for a moment, stops "letting ideas determine" (342) her behavior. Instead, she releases enough inhibitions to allow herself, out of love, to play physically with the aging Joe to obtain the erection he associates with youth and vitality. By literally carrying out the suggestion Joe made earlier (thereby uniting the physical with the spiritual and nature with civilization), Jill performs a gesture of love which includes — even as it transcends — a crudely sexual level. Due to her courage, their friendship of opposites attains a higher, more intimate level, free of the tension between the physical and spiritual which previously haunted it. By ironically becoming the teacher of the lesson Joe first taught her, she balances the cycle of gift giving between them in a way no gift bought with money could. Their newly cemented friendship is celebrated with a joyful laugh, a laugh which brings Joe back momentarily to his former self and makes Jill admit, from then on, "the humor in . . . errant lives" (315). When her friend passes away three years later, Jill knows the importance of not taking life too seriously, for she and Joe "had learned to laugh at everything that didn't make sense, which was everything important" (347).

The fine example set by Jill is contrasted by the pathetic one displayed by Hollywood superstar Sherry Solare. While Jill reaches out to people (including Sherry's own son) with her thoughtful and refined ways, Sherry ruthlessly manipulates those around her. Like a spoiled child whose ego needs are exacerbated by her powerful status as a major star, Sherry (like Jacy in *The Last Picture Show*) approaches life as a movie in which she constantly performs for the camera. For such a person, reality becomes hopelessly blurred with self-willed, self-serving illusions, making its inevitable messes impossible to tolerate. As Hollywood insider Jilly Legendre put it:

> "Sherry has only one thing: herself. She needs nothing else, believes in nothing else, knows nothing else. But she absolutely has to be pleased with herself: nothing can be wrong, and in order for nothing to be the whole world has to assume a certain shape. Everything else she knows and relates to in any way has to help keep the world tilted so that it reflects Sherry."
>
> "She's good at shoving the world around," he added. "She puts the camera where she wants it, and society and friendship and love are like the camera. She puts everything where she wants it, and as long as she can do that she's fine." (288)

But as Jilly goes on to point out, "Death is not a camera" (288). Therefore, when Sherry is faced with the ultimate mess she cannot control — the death of her son, Wynkyn — she self-destructs. As if in ironic payment for his mother's amorality, Wynkyn is accidentally shot by Sherry while she is in the midst of a sordid quarrel with her new lover, Owen, the opportunist who betrayed Jill. Eight months later, unable to cope with an event which would require her to admit the existence of a maternal obligation beyond her own ego, Sherry commits suicide in secluded material splendor "in her custom-made BMW, with the radio on, in her seven-car garage in Beverly Hills" (260).

Along with so many modern young people portrayed in McMurtry's fiction, Wynkyn lacked positive role models. His very name sounds like "win"/"kin" suggesting his urgent need for a normal family, something one cannot ironically "win" like a product on a game show. In contrast to his self-obsessed mother, Jill attempts, before his death, to address his needs. Realizing that "if there's a tragedy in Hollywood, it has to be the children" (227), she makes an effort to befriend Wynkyn and even manages to provide him with an evening away from the movie set. In the process, she enables him to experience a rare moment of transcendence by introducing him to the reality of nature, a world his mother compulsively avoids:

> We sat on the fence for half an hour, listening to the buffalo breathe. When the clouds hid the moon it would get so dark we could barely see the others, but we could hear them pulling hay out of the hayrack. Then the moon would come out again, very white, and we could see horns and even their shadows, and could smell the dusty hair of one underneath us. Wynkyn never moved. With the great sea of grass around us, the white moon, vast sky, and quiet beasts, we were both lifted out of our lives for a little time, and felt the

breath of the immemorial—maybe the only time Wynkyn had ever had such an experience (230).

In their lonely plight, McMurtry's young people often serve the function they do in Thomas Hardy's fiction, that of reflecting in their alienation the failure of adults.[9] In addition, however, McMurtry's children sometimes prove stronger than their adult counterparts, offering a Wordsworthian sense of spiritual redemption. This is the positive function they play at the end of *Some Can Whistle* and *Texasville*. Furthermore, the return to one's rural roots after having clearly outgrown them is another common device used by Hardy and McMurtry to dramatize the conflict between civilization and nature. But what distinguishes Hardy's *The Woodlanders*, a McMurtry favorite which uses this device, is the portrayal of civilization as a power more threatening than either fate or chance on the lives of people raised close to nature.[10] In *Texasville*, this threat is most clearly embodied by Jacy, a woman made fragile by worldly experience.

Texasville allows McMurtry to depict in Victorian fashion the moral growth experienced by Jacy Farrow in the thirty years since her appearance in *The Last Picture Show*. In contrast to her early confident self-absorption are the humility and self-awareness she has attained as a result of her experience in foreign movies, combined with the accidental death on a movie set of her six-year-old son (a clear parallel to Wynkyn). Her newfound stature is shown by the fact that her attempt to return to her simple Thalia roots forms the novel's center.

As they have for Jacy, the years since *The Last Picture Show* have been good for oilman Duane Moore in terms of outward success. Yet unlike her, the severe financial crisis of his business does not lead to the kind of focused soul-searching on his part which Jacy goes through in the process of grieving for her son. It is, therefore, inspiring that the tension in their now unconventional, platonic friendship ultimately leads Duane to a fuller appreciation of what is really important to his happiness: his family and his neglected role as potential nurturer. This spiritual awakening is hinted at when he physically awakens to discover Jacy swimming beside his fishing boat, for he is embarrassed at first by his inability to reconcile the real Jacy with his long-held idealization of her:

> His memories of the flirty girl she had been didn't go far towards describing the woman who looked at him from the brown lake. The swim goggles had left marks on her face. He remembered how vain she had once been, studying her face or body for the slightest blemish. She bruised easily, and though she liked wrestling and roughhousing, she had always scolded him fiercely if a bruise resulted.

Looking at her made him feel a little foolish — through the years he had been imagining her the most beautiful woman in the world, forgetting that those same years might have roughhoused with her more decisively and destructively than he ever had. (141)

Appropriately, the setting for this initial key meeting is an outdoor fishing lake, a striking change from the decadent swimming pool party for which Jacy once abandoned Duane.

In contrast to the willingness to grow, which Jacy and Duane embody, is Sonny, whose troubled initiation into manhood described in the earlier novel has ended in stagnation. For, in spite of owning a number of small businesses, he is increasingly obsessed with his past and unable to function effectively in the present. Through him, McMurtry dramatizes the modern danger, in an age of videocassette players and big-screen televisions, for individual withdrawal. The end of the novel finds him sitting in the bleachers overlooking the site of Thalia's history pageant, imagining himself about to perform a heroic act in an old Western. Blinded by enticing images in which right triumphs over despair, Sonny nearly jumps to his death (the ultimate form of human withdrawal) only to discover himself surrounded by the saving presence of his oldest friends — Duane, Karla, Jacy, and Ruth — and the morning dawn (558).

Texasville is filled with symbolic details which underscore the author's interest in the importance of balancing civilization with nature. The open and close of the novel are particularly memorable in this regard. As the story opens, Duane idly shoots at a pretentious two-story doghouse shaped to resemble a fort, an ironic reminder of his and Thalia's artificial escape from the frontier's hazards. Duane's dog, Shorty, which Jacy befriends as the novel progresses, confirms his symbolic closeness to nature by refusing to have anything to do with the phony doghouse (1). Furthermore, the dog's presence in the novel's last scene helps convey the idea of the periodic need to return to nature as an antidote for worldly success. In that scene, Jacy finally experiences a moment of spiritual renewal as she watches Duane's little boy and girl chase Shorty until he succeeds in making a mad dash for a resting spot under the BMW. The final symbolic image thus created of the dog resting under the car (nature under civilization) suggests the importance of the human being, however civilized or possessed of material things, remembering the underlying importance of nature from which he springs. Taking it a step further and viewing the children as youthful counterparts of Jacy and Duane, the scene optimistically implies the indelible strength of nature despite man's attempts to conquer it. In this contest, Duane's closing words regarding Shorty — "I don't think he plans to make a run for it" — are comforting in their suggestion that nature's presence is still there whenever man's sophisticated fantasies or selfish follies threaten his sanity (561).

Other examples of nature symbolism which threaten to undercut Duane and Jacy's civilized ennui (which is worthy of Thomas Hardy) involve the pageant laboriously created to celebrate Thalia's history. Jacy's claim to movie fame arose from playing Jungla in Italian Tarzan pictures, so it comes as little surprise when she leaps at the chance to play Eve to Duane's reluctant Adam. Though in her youth Jacy played roles opposite Duane to fulfill her ego at the expense of others, now she does so with a sense of moral obligation and a realization of the importance of role models in the lives of ordinary people unable to appreciate the emptiness behind success. While, for people watching, the Eden she and Duane recreate as Thalia's golden couple may suggest the material rewards and outward beauty they embody, for Jacy, Eden now lies in reality's potential for spiritual renewal. The unexpected way the pageant ends (with adults being pelted with eggs by kids) is also symbolically appropriate, for the neglected children make their presence known by eggs associated with nature's fertility and redemptive power over those (such as Duane and Jacy) jaded with the adult world of civilization. Not surprisingly, in light of McMurtry's negative view of organized religion, the first onslaught of eggs hits the fundamentalist preacher G. G., who mistakenly concludes that they come as punishment from God (530).

In *Texasville* and *Somebody's Darling*, McMurtry shows what happens to modern civilized characters who become too removed from nature: They either seek a healthy balance or become miserable and self-destruct. These are the works of a man deeply divided between his worldly success as a writer and his simple rural heritage. And why not? After all, for all the potential comforting peace and security civilization may provide, especially for the culturally inclined and the disadvantaged, it is at best a deadly reductive peace which in some ways inevitably isolates (much as language, however wonderful at expressing ideas, can never do more than hint at reality's true complexity and vitality). These are major concerns, and while McMurtry presents no easy answers for reconciliation between nature and civilization, between his and our country's past and present, his fiction does, in true Victorian fashion, find hope in the confrontation of such problems with personal courage and the possibility of moments of transcendence shared with others. And if one takes Augustus's example in *Lonesome Dove* as a guide (or the endings of *Somebody's Darling* and *Texasville*), then the answer, however difficult today, lies in a constant civilized striving for accommodation between the id-like selfish demands of nature and the potentially over-repressive and reductive forces associated with civilization. This hard answer is the thoughtful response of a man committed to working out his personal tensions, a man who refuses, like Danny Deck, to either run from the truth or remain in the swirling waters of confusion and oblivion.

CHAPTER FOUR

"Angels near the Star"

THE SEARCH FOR TRANSCENDENCE

> *He made the proposal with cheerful energy; he was hardly the same man as the man of the small dark hours. Even among the moodiest the tendency to be cheered is stronger than the tendency to be cast down; and a soul's specific gravity constantly re-asserts itself as less than that of the sea of troubles into which it is thrown.*
> —Thomas Hardy, *The Woodlanders*

THE END OF *Horseman, Pass By* finds Lonnie in a country church, alienated from those around him as he seeks a basis for transcendence. The temporary relief from the pain of isolation he finally experiences comes neither from his family nor the phony words said by the preacher, but from a talented singer who puts him in an elevated spiritual state reminiscent of the Victorian ethic of enthusiasm. Walter E. Houghton, quoting John Stuart Mill, describes this phenomenon as

> that higher state of mind, in which the selfish desires of the ego, far from having to be conquered by the moral will, are swept aside by the selfless impulse of the "noble" emotions, in a state of enthusiasm. And though in itself ephemeral, it has lasting effects. By "winding up to a high pitch those feelings of an elevated kind which are already in character," the "exciting enthusiasm" of music gives them "a glow and a fervor, which, though transitory at its utmost height, is precious for sustaining them at other times." (263–64)

Houghton adds that the ethic of enthusiasm assumes that the "organ of virtue is sensibility rather than conscience" (264) and was inherited from the Romantics and their "Rousseauistic faith in the goodness of human nature and the spontaneous flowering of the moral sentiments, as long as they were uncorrupted by the 'evil' influences of civilization and unrestrained by authoritarian discipline" (267). He gives as an example these lines from Wordsworth's *The Excursion:* "We live by Admiration, Hope, and Love/ And even as these are well and wisely fixed/ In dignity of being we ascend" (267).

When Larry McMurtry wrote his short story entitled, "Angels near the Star: A Prelude to Remembrance," he was still in college. Although an early formative work, it captures in many ways the moral philosophy and attitude toward art which underlie the author's later fiction. For, like the Victorians who questioned the value of traditional Christianity and advocated a doctrine of humanity in its place, McMurtry's fiction, starting with "Angels," advocates a religious philosophy of inspired personal growth based on the search for transcendent moments. In his fictional portrayal of organized religion, the author will suggest, along with John Stuart Mill, that it nourishes an "essentially selfish character" (Houghton 284). Like Edward Dowden, McMurtry will repeatedly imply that men must seek "for a natural rather than a miraculous or traditional foundation for morality" (289).

Appropriately, a scene with parallels to the conclusion of *Horseman, Pass By* forms the basis of "Angels near the Star." Also set in a church, it begins with the theme of the individual's relation to others, as the narrator describes a young man seated apart from the crowd while the organist begins to play a prelude: "One person heard and smiled, and knew it not. He was very young, only 19, and he was occupying the pew farthest from the pulpit. He always did, for in it he was free to enjoy church in his own unique fashion. Here, he could dream unassailed, for the minister was nearsighted, and the choir self-occupied. All else he could scrutinize without detection" (1).

The young man cherishes isolation, for it protects his ability and desire to dream without encountering others' disapproval. As his eyes roam about the church, he sees nature in the "arched ceiling," which resembles a "resting cloud." And as he proceeds to enter his private reverie, a kaleidoscope of images follows, mixing nature, civilization, and religion.

> Time, toiling time, was naught and contents of the empty eons, the hordes of human experience were opened for his imagination to pluck . . . Ancient Athens, the Athens of the Acropolis . . . the amazing Alcemonindae and Alcibiades flowed forth. . . . The seven hills beside the Tiber, home to

Romulus and the wolf . . . the glory of Genesis and the first six words therein
came to mind, and a vision of Ruth in the corn, murmuring, "Whither thou
diest will I die, and there will I be buried." . . . Plunging from the heights to
the fetching vision of a girl's elfish grin as she peeked on their doubles good-
night kiss. . . . The white-haired Wordsworth, penning his "Prelude" to the
music of England's lakes and larks. . . . The hoary, hallowed hands of
Schweitzer, in a gloomy hut in a gloomy land, pushing back the gloom with
the magic of an organ prelude. . . . A prelude like a prayer, and a saintly
white-haired pillar of peace and power.[1] (1, 2)

Here are hints of the thematic concerns which will inform the author's
later fiction. His interest in civilization is represented by "Ancient Athens,
the Athens of the Acropolis," his fascination with rivers by "the amazing
Alcemonidae and Alcibiades," his interest in religion and the process of
creation by the first words of Genesis, and his concern with the human
potential for loyalty, love, and courage even in the face of death by the
biblical character of Ruth (a forerunner of Ruth in *The Last Picture Show*).
In addition, there are two civilized white-haired historical figures who represent contrasting relations with nature reminiscent of Gus and Call:
Wordsworth, who finds inspiration in nature and grounds for his vision of
the poet as godlike creator, and Albert Schweitzer, a man determined to
dominate the dark jungles of nature by flooding them with the light of civilization.

As "Angels near the Star" continues, it puts the theme of the relation of
the individual to others in a moral context. The young man, having en-
joyed his solitary meditation, exchanges smiles with the female choir
leader, reminding himself in the process of people's moral responsibility to
acknowledge and validate each other.

"My friend!" he thought, and was happy in the knowledge that he was right.
She was his friend, and Sunday was barren without that brief exchange of
reassuring smiles. Once, in a very foul mood, he had failed to return the
tribute, but had peered at the floor in stony unconcern. That stubbornness
remained yet as one of those excruciating painful memories which haunt us
ever so often. As is always the case, he tried to put it aside at once, but the
agony had run its brief course. (2)

Soon, the minister begins to speak. McMurtry's distrust of language
and its attendant reductive qualities versus the solid reality of nature (a
conflict later developed in *All My Friends Are Going to Be Strangers* and *Lonesome Dove*) is dramatized by the boy's failure to hear the minister's words
because of his interest in the good man's soul, which he visualizes using
images from nature:

The boy did not hear the words, so engrossed was he in the man. A native, a friend . . . a teacher . . . a confessor; all of these the minister was. It did not matter to the boy that he'd heard the words before, or that he heard them not at all, for the message sped clear as the evening bugle over shrouded hills from the old man's soul. His character was his oration, warm tranquil as a valley lake. . . . For him no winds of doubt. (3)

And the boy thinks "here's religion's essence." The author's anger regarding religious hypocrisy (so forcefully manifested in *The Last Picture Show*) is next conveyed using the minister as a moral yardstick. "Half of the people in this church have his tranquillity and humility to some degree, the other half think they do, and how easy it is to tell which" (3).

Next, McMurtry's interest in the individual's search for transcendent moments and their importance to his or her spiritual life is revealed as the boy recalls

two soul sating experiences when his spirit had had "wings as eagles" and he had soared secure with God and the seraphim for a brief space. . . . He wondered interminably what had produced that ecstasy, akin to pain, that had caused him to tremble. . . . He knew who but still he wondered how and why. He would dearly love to find a formula for producing the feeling more often, but he knew that he might as well search for the Cities of Cibola. Still, he hoped that he would be blessed again and until then he had his memories to keep him hoping. (3)

Note that the mystery of how such transcendent moments with God come about remains unclear, oblivious to the spiritually hungry individual's attempts to produce them consciously or capture their secret (an idea later dramatized by Ruth's similar realization in *The Last Picture Show*). Yet the memory of such moments provides a solid foundation for the hope and strength to endure hardships over time (an idea recalling Wordsworth's "spots of time" in *The Prelude*).[2]

Then the boy experiences another such moment, a moment at once magically enriched with a "sound like the angels near a solitary star," yet firmly based on the people around him, among whom there "was home like heaven, and seraphim, and love" in addition to "the friendly hands and peace like the sleep during a quiet rain . . . and the friends, their voices warm, sincerity as deep as the coloured velvet on which shone the dull gold cross" (4). Like the scene McMurtry many years later wrote for *Texasville*, in which the broken and fragile Sonny suddenly finds himself safely surrounded by friends, so an important part of the young man's uplifting experience in the earlier story comes from the close proximity of people he believes love him. Ironically, because he is an artist, this intense feeling of oneness arises largely from the exercise of his singular imagination.

Finally, in a key passage, the narrator states that the boy "knew his God was a dreamer too, and would understand . . . and oh what a dreamer was He. . . . For he dreamt of a sunny earth and mighty universe where love and friends and stars watched by angels were common . . . oh the Beauty his dream had created" (5). And so McMurtry conveniently portrays the boy as absolving himself of any pain or guilt produced by an artist's lonely alienation, for God is, in fact, a dreamer like himself, a dreamer who not only does not condemn, but actually approves of the author's dreams. "But our father God dreamed and did and so, thought the lad, should I" (5). (McMurtry's idea here again echoes Wordsworth's *The Prelude*, most notably its climactic scene on Mount Snowden when, under "starry heavens," the poet comes face to face with a "mind that feeds upon infinity. . . . A mind sustained by recognition of transcendent power.")[3]

The conclusion of "Angels near the Star" involves a boy and girl under the stars on a summer night, a scene of transcendent power for the participants (and quoted at length in Chapter 2 for its parallels to *The Last Picture Show*'s depiction of Sonny and Ruth's first kiss). This final vignette underscores how moments of great joy experienced by individuals, often in relation to others, serve as the basis for an ongoing faith in a spiritual realm which contrasts with the constant changes and hardships of being human. As if to stress this point, the boy as a young artist has a difficult time momentarily giving up either his dreams or the church he associates with them: "then the moment, gone, and gone, oh gone thence forever, but left was faith that time would hence more. . . . And he thought its faith that God will ever bring such beauties and such Good that's faith by which ye shall live alone" (6). And so he lingers "loath to leave for so long the cool quiet peace and the untroubled thought and deathless dreams. Without lay the fiery sun, and the troubles, torments, uncertainties, problems, confusions, ecstasies, yearnings, and strife he must face" (6, 7).

The personal religious faith based on individual striving so strongly celebrated in McMurtry's early story is further confirmed by a brief examination of his college letters, written about the same time. In a letter to Mike Kunkel accompanying the story, for example, the author notes that the story is his "most autobiographical." In another letter, he writes that he finds "the Brahmin religion one of the most beautiful."[4] Other letters further convey his inability to accept blind dogma over a religion based on the concept of personal growth and enthusiasm. In a letter dated two months after the one containing "Angels" (December 3, 1955), the author declares:

> Doubts are very necessary to forming a firm belief. To hold a belief without doubts is to assume infallibility. Even if the belief is true, it is most likely not wholly true, and can only benefit by collusion with error. And if it's wholly true, to hold it so above question soon reduces it to dogma. Religion (dig this philosophy man) must be personal, I don't care what the churches say. I fear it will be awhile before I reach the heights of religious passion I hit in Angels Near The Star [*sic*]. I drifted a far piece, not from God, but from orthodoxy.

And finally, in a letter dated August 31, 1956, McMurtry boldly asserts that he does not believe

1. that Jesus Christ was Divine,
2. that there is likely to be a hereafter,
3. or that God is necessarily either Triene or anthropomorphic to any degree.

Yet he goes on to state, "That doesn't cripple my spirituality or personal sense of religion . . . but it pretty well cuts the heart out of contemporary Christianity."

The distrust of fundamentalists expressed in McMurtry's college letters is also seen in Lonnie's disillusionment found at the close of *Horseman, Pass By*. Critics such as Gordon Bennett Smith have rightly read the church scene as an expression of hostility. But too often overlooked is how it may also be read as a powerful expression of McMurtry's moral and spiritual values.

Like the boy in "Angels," Lonnie sees the church both in terms of those he loves and of nature's beauty. Upon entering the church, Lonnie thinks: "But anyhow, it was dark in the church, and the deep-blue glass windows were cool as shady water. I always liked those blue windows, and I liked the rich brown wood of the church seats, wood that was the color of Halmea's breasts" (166). However, unlike the boy in the earlier story, Lonnie's powerful assertion of his own personal moral values verges on the heroic, for they are undercut at every turn by outward circumstances. For him, this is no ordinary Sunday, but the funeral of his beloved grandfather (appropriately named Homer as a metaphor for civilization),[5] whom his amoral stepuncle shot. For this reason, Lonnie cannot indulge the luxury of blithely ignoring the preacher's words (who, unlike the preacher in "Angels", is not a positive role model) and pursue a "deathless dream," but instead must take each word as a betrayal of the positive feelings for his grandfather, whom he holds in his heart. Listening to the strange preacher read Homer Bannon's background from a cue card, Lonnie realizes that he "went on and told a lot that wasn't true about Granddad and the church. He told some more that wasn't true about Granddad's being respected and hardly anybody cared much for Granddad. Some hated his guts. Me and a few cowmen and a few hands and an old-timer or two loved and respected him" (168). Circumstances also dictate that Lonnie cannot view church as a positive source of community, but instead as a place where people temporarily pretend a sense of unity out of hypocrisy:

> Then the old ladies from Thalia trooped in, whispering to one another and shaking powder on the aisles. . . . More people came than Granddad would ever have dreamed of having: store people and business and oil drillers and strangers by the swarm. People were at the funeral Granddad hadn't ever seen. Some were there that he'd forgotten, and some that he hated and despised. Their wives were with them, all wearing slick black dresses, with little veils hanging down over their eyes and white gloves on their hands. (167)

Adding to Lonnie's frustration, he cannot sit apart enjoying the isolation of a dreamer (as did the boy in "Angels"), but must join his stepuncle Hud and his sickly grandmother at the front of the church. In fact, his only relief during the service (when he thinks he and his grandfather are validated) comes from the artistry of a woman who "sang solos for everything, but she practiced her singing, and was good at it" (168). Using the artistry of civilization to sing a song about nature—"Yes, We'll Gather at the River"—she gives Lonnie his longed-for moment of transcendence:

> While she was singing I wasn't mad, and my eyes got hot and I had to wipe wetness away with my fingers. She made the song go higher and higher, and as long as it lasted everything was different, and I thought again that Granddad might be moving above the pastures. I saw the river, running down the canyon and out under the trees, with cattle standing in it, and horses watering at the pools. It was a sight Granddad always loved, a flowing river. (169)

Lonnie's moment of inspiration quickly evaporates as the funeral service continues with a sermon delivered by Brother Barstow. A preacher despised by Lonnie (and Homer when he was alive), Barstow provides another focal point for McMurtry's anger over small-town religious hypocrisy. Ironically portraying himself as Homer's close friend, the minister's shameless disregard for the truth fills Lonnie with disgust. Even when Brother Barstow rightly stresses Homer's close connection to the land, he proves that he misunderstands the value of the man's work ethic when he declares, "God has taken him, taken him where he will never have to labor in the sun and the sleet again" (171).

Before Lonnie can leave the church, he must endure yet another disturbing moment as he passes the open coffin. Its inappropriate pink satin lining is only topped by the artificial feminine makeup that Lonnie notices covering Homer's face. McMurtry's concern with the sterile, feminizing aspects of civilization is conveyed here, relieved only by Lonnie's squeezing of the songbook linked with the redemptive power of art:

> They had a slick black suit on him, and a white shirt and a vest, and a dark red necktie with a little gold bird on it. His hands were on his chest, as white as paint. I squeezed the songbook when I looked at his face. They had put paint on him, like a woman wears, red paint. I could see it on his cheeks, and caked around his mouth. I could see slick oil on his hair, and some stuff like honey around his eye. (172)

Not surprisingly, Lonnie tears away from the crowd as soon as he leaves the church, clutching his songbook and thinking, "I wasn't going any further with that crowd, Hud or no Hud" (173). Finding at last a private spot beneath a hedge, he searches his hymnbook for "the song about the beautiful river" (173) but has no luck finding it. Trying to recapture the moment of peace he experienced earlier in church, he recalls how beautifully the singer performed and soon pictures getting up early mornings to watch his grandfather ride out to work in the pasture. He realizes that Homer "had passed me finally and for good, to go to his land" (173). Returning the songbook to the church, he lingers outside it, "looking at the grass, at the skim-milk clouds, at those blue church-house windows, thinking of the horseman that had passed" (174).

Lonnie's personal moment of transcendence, which recalls McMurtry's college story, is essential preparation for the character's radical next step: the seeking out of a new, more civilized community. For, while the boy's isolation in "Angels near the Star" is largely that of the artist, Lonnie's isolation is more explicitly a moral one, making the self-imposed removal from the community he has always known a fitting culmination of his relations to people depicted earlier. From the novel's beginning, he appears as a lonely, sensitive, caring individual, confused by Hud's insensitivity and amorality while at the same time responsive to his grandfather's love, as well as that shown him by the sensuous black cook, Halmea. Within this context, two events caused by Hud — Halmea's rape and Homer's apparent murder — force him to fight to maintain his inner integrity and moral sensibility. When he views Halmea's rape, he experiences confusion, for it excites him sexually even as it morally repulses him:

> I was thinking how I wanted to do good things for Halmea and never do a mean thing to her, but I couldn't get over wanting to wallow her. I thought of her that day she brought the lemonade and set it by the bed when I felt sick; and I remembered the streak of flour had been white on her forehead. I wanted to thank her for that and do something nice for her on account of it. But even thinking about the lemonade, what I remembered most, more than the tall sweaty glass or the icy juice or her cool fingers on my forehead, was the dark tight tops of her breasts as she stooped over. Thinking of all that made me want to cry, and I turned over again and wished I could find a way to get peace. I wished I could get together with Halmea somewhere off from the ranch, where we could just talk. If we could, I might think of a way to let her know all the different things I thought about her that night; maybe she would have known what was silly about them, and what was right and good. (118)

Even more disturbing, after discovering that Hud shot Homer, Lonnie experiences a sense of isolation and a sudden deadening of all feeling for others — a frightening suggestion of the cold indifference to humanity he must combat to retain his soul: "I dried up then. I felt like I didn't have anything else to say, to Hud or anybody, ever. I was just pushed back in myself like a two-bit variety-store telescope" (160).

Therefore, when Lonnie abandons Hud and his home, it is not simply out of insensitivity or escapism (as some critics have suggested)[6] — rather, he leaves in order to preserve his own moral integrity and out of respect for Halmea and Homer. In addition, his leaving suggests his quest for a larger and presumably more civilized world.[7] This is not merely appropriate, but a relief, for with Homer's death the Bannon ranch has become a symbol, not only of a dying way of life, but of such a life's ultimate moral corruption. It is in this context that Lonnie's reading *From Here to Eternity*[8] early on will become prophetic, for it identifies him as one who will seek to transcend his environment. *Horseman, Pass By*'s final sentence emphasizes Lonnie's gentle yet unbroken spirit, as well as his determination to enlarge the scope of his community: "The cab was dark and the dash light threw shadows across his face, so that when I looked at him, he reminded me of someone that I cared for, he reminded me of everyone I knew" (179).

In McMurtry's first novel, the moral values suggested by "Angels" are effectively dramatized. His sympathetic portrayal of Lonnie forcefully contrasts positive values of love, empathy, loyalty, and courage with the devastatingly harmful effects of cruel and selfish behavior arising from self-hatred and social frustration. A youth of heightened sensibility, Lonnie further illustrates the author's faith in the redemptive power of transcendental moments associated with others which art, rightfully used, may help provide. This faith provides a striking contrast to his suspicion of organized religion and its potential for hypocrisy, repression, and stunted growth. McMurtry's complex response to religion would continue to inform both the form and content of his later fiction. For example, just as "Angels" hovers in the background of *Horseman, Pass By*, so in *The Last Picture Show* the author's condemnation of organized religion is balanced by his belief in transcendental moments which sustain the individual in his or her civilized quest for meaning and growth.

Early in the novel, McMurtry includes an exchange between the preacher's son, Joe Bob, and his English teacher which contains an important implied commentary on religion. In reference to Keats's poem "Ode to a Nightingale," Joe Bob asserts, "It sounded like he wanted to be a nightingale, and I think it's silly for all these poets to want to be something besides what the Lord made them" (32). His teacher, Mr. Cecil, patiently replies, "Oh, I don't think he wanted to be a nightingale, Joe Bob. . . . Maybe he just wanted to be immortal" (33). To which Joe Bob responds, "All you have to do to be immortal is lead a good Christian life" (33). The moment illustrates McMurtry's view that religion must be personal (as suggested in one of his college letters)[9] and involves striving for individual growth to achieve moments of transcendence, as opposed to self-satisfied assurances of immortality based on empty rhetoric. Furthermore, the situation recalls Matthew Arnold's remarks in *Culture and Anarchy* concerning the dual roles of culture and religion. Both, he contends, deal with human perfection in terms of man's internal condition,[10] but while culture involves "becoming something rather than in having something," organized religion too often encourages self-satisfied stasis as opposed to continual growth.[11] After his exchange with Joe Bob, Mr. Cecil chooses to read aloud to him Keats's famous poem "Ode on a Grecian Urn," an ironically appropriate choice in part because of its link with the Greek culture which inspires Arnold and because it emphasizes man's mortal state as one of constant change, rather than cold stasis.

The contrasting approaches to faith represented by Joe Bob and Mr. Cecil are dramatized by other characters in *The Last Picture Show*. Chapter 2 mentioned Ruth Popper's major role as a moral paradigm resulting partly from her brave search for the transcendent in the form of "the beautiful thing . . . the whole moment toward which all sharp little individual moments tended" (101). Set against this search for personal growth are those stunted individuals, such as Joe Bob and Jacy, who have mindlessly become addicted to organized religion or dreams of Hollywood as harmful substitutes for growth. Like the major Victorian novelists, McMurtry portrays the individual's search for meaning largely through his or her relationships with others. And nothing stands more in the way of such a pursuit as a solipsistic preoccupation with an inherited theology or the narcissistic imitation of a Hollywood star.

Gordon Bennett Smith demonstrates great insight in his description of the connection between Joe Bob's social victimization and his bizarre behavior at the end of the novel, when he kidnaps a little girl on the very day he is to preach his second sermon. The young man's behavior logically results from the town's unconscious hostility toward preachers combined with the unhealthy repression instilled by Joe Bob's father. In Smith's words:

> He [Joe Bob] has little chance for finding the "normal life" that he seeks, for his father has disabled him from recognizing the basic normality that is already his. All too human and vulnerable from the start, Joe Bob has been so put in the way of his desires that he develops perversions and surrenders to them, partially as an unconscious escape from a world he can no longer endure. Church religion does not help Joe Bob; it destroys him. (64)

Smith is also on the mark as he analyzes the town's hypocrisy in condemning Joe Bob for not molesting the girl once he kidnapped her:

> He [Joe Bob] is whipsawed between the town's sectarian morality and its appreciation of *machismo*. The crowd explains his not having violated Molly in the pejorative phrase, "preacher's boy." Joe Bob's closeness to religion is associated with deficient masculinity. The modern assumptions of the townspeople do not allow for distinctions between the absence of heterosexual drive and the deliberate squelching of such a drive by a preacher (65, 66).

Through McMurtry's highly sympathetic portrayal of Joe Bob's pathetic plight, he effectively condemns the harmful effects on sexuality and self-esteem the repressiveness associated with organized religion may induce. In such a situation, perverse regressive sexual behavior releases the victim from the pressure of a limiting social role.

Though she does not exhibit the extreme behavior of Joe Bob or suffer the social ostracism he endures, Jacy Farrow is another example of arrested growth. Selfish and narcissistic, her values are derived from Hollywood rather than organized religion. Early on McMurtry explicitly asserts the equation of movies with religion in Jacy's life through his description of her bedroom: "Next to the picture of Duane was an alarm clock and a white zipper Bible, and on the other side of the bed was Jacy's pile of movie magazines, most of them with Debbie Reynolds on the cover. Debbie Reynolds was Jacy's ideal" (40). McMurtry further shows the fallacy of blindly following Hollywood's hedonistic values when Jacy meets her match in Abilene. An oil driller who comes looking for her mother while Lois is ironically visiting Joe Bob in jail, Abilene treats Jacy like a sex toy in order to get back at her mother. In the process, Jacy experiences the loss of individuality and the spiritual worthlessness which inevitably result from a value system based on treating humans merely as commodities to be used and thrown away:

> He was just going on, absorbed in himself, moving, nudging, thrusting— she was no more than an object. She wanted to protest that, but before she could she began to lose sight of herself, lose hold of herself. She was rolled this way and that, into feelings she hadn't known, hadn't expected, couldn't avoid. She lost all thought of doing anything, she was completely lost to herself. He played her out as recklessly as he had played the final ball, and when he did she scattered as the red balls had scattered when the white one struck them so hard. (174)

McMurtry's condemnation of organized religion, coupled with his belief in transcendental moments, underlies not only his first and third novels, but also his second, *Leaving Cheyenne*. It is the story of Molly and the two favorite men in her life, Gid and Johnny—neither of whom she marries—over the course of their lives. Molly's willingness to fly in the face of convention and love unconditionally—a trait McMurtry celebrates— ironically causes her to lose one of her sons to the church.

The author's firm belief that religion must be personal is dramatized by Molly's confrontation with Jimmy, her illegitimate son by Gid, as he reaches manhood. Her unwillingness to address the church on its own terms illustrates the simple dignity which may result from reliance upon one's own feelings while recognizing the reductive quality of words:

> "Fornication and adultery is what you did, Momma," he said.
> I guess what he wanted was for me to deny it, to tell him I hadn't really done neither one, and that everything the preacher said about me was wrong. I sat the peas on the table.
> "Jimmy, those are just two words to me," I said. "Even if they do come out of the Bible."
> "But you did them," he said. "In this house we're living in, too."
> "I wasn't saying I didn't," I said. "And I wasn't saying I'm good. I guess I'm terrible. But words is one thing and loving a man is another thing; that's

all I can say about it." And that was true. The words didn't describe what I had lived with Gid, or with Johnny, at all; they didn't describe what we had felt. But Jimmy hadn't felt it, so I couldn't tell him that and make him understand." (196)

Sadly, Jimmy does not share his mother's ability to trust in the validity of personal feelings. As a result, he allows society, and particularly the church, to turn him against her, and himself in the process. For not only do the church's rigid teachings repress Jimmy and his natural love for his mother, but through the exploitative sexual abuse he endures from a male Sunday school teacher who serves as a father figure, his own sexuality ironically becomes perverted. As Gordon Bennett Smith writes: "Religion has turned Jimmy against heterosexual expression in its doctrinaire condemnation of the kind of extramarital relations which produced his illegitimacy, yet it cannot conquer the fact of Jimmy's sexuality, which takes a homosexual channel of expression" (37). Smith goes on to state that "the love and forgiveness that Christianity is supposed to produce has been drowned in the self-hatred and perversity that it really has produced" (36).

Set against the harmful effects of organized religion in the novel is the inspiring example of the enduring friendship between Molly, Gid, and Johnny, a friendship punctuated by many wonderful moments. It culminates in a transcendent one for Johnny following Gid's death at the novel's conclusion. Alone on his friend's ranch "watching that white moon circling out over Gid's pastures" (297), he starts an imaginary dialogue with Gid during which they debate their respective competence and compare material assets. Finally, Johnny poses the central question behind the male banter: "Which one of us was satisfied?" From what Johnny calls the "Great Perhaps," Gid immediately responds, "Hell, that's easy. . . . Neither one. We neither one married her, did we?" (298). Through the novel's bittersweet conclusion, McMurtry shows how death reinforces the importance of love over material concerns or societal expectations.

In his first three novels, McMurtry attacked the organized religion of small Texas towns and subtly advocated in its place a value system (similar to that expressed in "Angels") based on concern for others, transcendental moments, and individual striving for personal growth. Following *The Last Picture Show,* the author abruptly turned away from organized religion as a primary target. As he continued to mature personally and professionally, his focus increasingly fell on the conflict between civilization and nature and the endless quest for personal affirmation in a society lacking transcendental values. A good example of how the latter subject is treated in McMurtry's more recent fiction can be found in *The Desert Rose.* At the center of the novel is a middle-aged Las Vegas showgirl named Harmony, who reflects upon and oversees the story's action. As her name suggests, McMurtry embodies, through her, his faith in the capacity of the human spirit for renewal and achievement of personal peace over time, despite hardships and loss.

Critical to Harmony's optimistic spirit (and the author's) is the potentially positive role of dreams. Early in the novel, Harmony's cynical daughter, Pepper, asks her, "How come you're such a dreamer?" (30). Harmony does not reply but instead thinks that she "didn't know, you were or you weren't so far as that went" (30). Indeed, she is a dreamer, for she is constantly reflecting upon people — past and present — and silently wishing the best for them. Though lacking the brilliant imagination and sophistication of the artist, she is, nonetheless (like Lonnie in *Horseman, Pass By*), a legitimate heir to the long line of constructive dreamers in McMurtry's fiction (beginning with "Angels") for whom the author has a particular fondness. In this context, it is little wonder that McMurtry has publicly admitted that he was inspired by writing *The Desert Rose* and even declared that his heroine taught him, "Hope is a form of courage."[12]

In "Angels near the Star," McMurtry wrote, "But our father God dreamed and did and so, thought the lad, should I." Harmony dreams, without knowing why, and in the process provides a moral framework which transcends much of life's sordidness. Unlike Jacy in *The Last Picture Show,* Sherry in *Somebody's Darling* or even her own daughter Pepper, Harmony's constant unselfish involvement with others gives her a realistic perspective on dreams which enhances rather than destroys her ability to deal with reality. Her maturity in this regard is all the more remarkable when one considers that she makes her living creating a larger than life illusion for an audience, a fragile illusion based on physical beauty. The novel's opening underscores her strength in this regard as, driving eastward out of Las Vegas, she thinks, "But then dreams, they weren't too real — or maybe real but not too likely to happen" (10). Her resolve is suddenly tested when, after being fired from her job, she imagines it was all a dream, but then immediately realizes, "that explanation was looking on the bright side, which was important, but just not always true. Sometimes the truth lay on the other side from the bright side, which was where it lay in this case" (179).

Harmony's inspiration, then, comes not from denying reality, but in finding an accommodating balance between its frequent harshness and the sustaining power of dreams. One such dream is that of her husband, Ross, a sweet man in her eyes even though he deserted her when Pepper was just a little girl. A romantic by nature, Harmony "had never seen anything wrong with being romantic, it just meant you were a little more tender about things and liked to think about the good kinds of things that could happen rather than the bad kinds of things, which there were enough of, there was no point in dwelling on them" (17). In part because they are simply put, Harmony's words form an easy target for ridicule in an age filled with cynicism, but in point of fact, her positive attitude ironically echoes McMurtry's own regarding the proper role of art: "I have come to want of [art] more or less what Matthew Arnold wanted: that is, that it perform a function once the trust of religion, that of reconciling us to our experience. I want an art that . . . redeems the experience it presents; the last thing I want is an art that idly documents discontents and as idly adds them to my own" (*Film Flam* 44).

In contrast to the positive role McMurtry believes art should play is the negative role organized religion adopts when it encourages a world view of fear and pessimism. In *The Desert Rose,* McMurtry sets off Harmony's innocent optimism against a fashionable judgmental attitude of despair among ironically religious people in Las Vegas who

> seemed to think the end of the world was probably going to come in a year or two. . . . Gary said all those views were nonsense. It wasn't that he didn't believe in God, he just felt there was no reason to suppose the end of the world was at hand particularly, which Harmony agreed with, it seemed to her why should it be?, maybe people who thought otherwise were not reading the Bible right or something. (23)

Just as the exchange between Joe Bob and Mr. Cecil in *The Last Picture Show* illustrated McMurtry's and Arnold's belief in the importance of culture over organized religion, so Harmony's constant faith celebrates McMurtry's belief in the potential power of dreams over traditional religion's failure to inspire. The simple wisdom of her faith is confirmed by the novel's conclusion when she takes a brave personal journey to be reconciled to a new unknown life with her long estranged husband, Ross, a life which, whatever it ultimately holds, will be buoyed by her gift for optimism.

A character in the novel who reinforces much of Harmony's ability to get the most out of life is Mel, the wealthy and eccentric former fashion photographer to whom her daughter becomes engaged. McMurtry's interest in the necessity of being able to discern the spiritual reality which lies beneath appearances is reflected in the skillful way he initially creates a sense of mystery surrounding Mel. Because the reader's introduction to the character consists of Pepper's and her friend Buddy's early impressions in the context of Mel's creating nude videos, it is initially easy to dismiss him merely as a perverted exploiter of young bodies. But by quickly demonstrating his essential moral integrity and genuine artistic sensibility, McMurtry cleverly puts the reader in the same role the optimistic Harmony adopts throughout the novel, that of being able to see beyond sordid appearances to the good which may be found in the human soul. Furthermore, in terms of Pepper's world, Mel ironically becomes the artist as moral creator or secular God foreshadowed in "Angels near the Star." For not only does he transform Pepper's physical world with things of beauty, more importantly he provides a moral, spiritual dimension which her life has sorely lacked (as evidenced by his thoughtful attempts to reconcile her with her mother). With this in mind, his original voyeuristic videotaping of Pepper and Buddy could suggest an asexual God looking down on Adam and Eve in fascination and appreciation of their beauty. Little wonder that McMurtry has written, "It was hardly just that [Pepper] should find someone as considerate as Mel, but there you are. . . ."[13]

Larry McMurtry has always believed in juxtaposing the vulgarity of man's physical existence with his potential for the transcendent. While *The Desert Rose* may lack the scope of his other novels, he shows more clearly in it the rewarding of the search for the transcendent. It is easy to see in this context the appropriateness of the novel's title, for even in the most arid of moral climates, the author finds grounds for hope.

A continuing thread running through all of McMurtry's work to date is a fervent advocacy of the potentially redemptive effects of civilization, with its links to art and dreams despite their inherent dangers (including the tendency to remove the individual from the reality of nature). For even when strongly attacking the sterile decadence of Hollywood dreammakers in *Somebody's Darling,* for example, McMurtry makes clear the possibility for civilized individuals like Jill and Joe to transcend their environment through honest commitment to each other and maintaining contacts with nature. Similarly, in contrast to his harsh attack against organized religion in *The Last Picture Show,* McMurtry applauds the civilized humanity of the down-to-earth Sam the Lion and Ruth Popper for offering sources of hope for others like Sonny and Billy in society. And in the author's first novel, *Horseman, Pass By,* all the primitive, brutal inhumanity displayed by Hud can drive away, but not destroy, the civilized sensibility of the rural Lonnie, who responds to the church soloist in his search for transcendence. A look at *Anything for Billy* can further illustrate the close connection that exists between the benefits of civilization and the power of dreams despite

McMurtry's ambivalence toward both. A scene from *All My Friends Are Going to Be Strangers* provides an appropriate introduction, a novel whose narrative voice foreshadows that of the later novel.

Perhaps Danny Deck's noblest moment in *All My Friends* occurs when he throws Geoffrey, Godwin's obnoxious hustler, off a balcony. The incident is a dramatic example of the author's belief in the need to preserve the best of civilization — despite its limitations — from bullying barbarians and maintain it as a haven of kindness and decency. Before his act, Danny watches in disgust as Geoffrey sadistically bullies Godwin, a distinguished British sociology professor, for money. Standing out on the balcony seconds later and staring up at the stars (a McMurtry symbol of transcendence), Danny, in a moment of insight, realizes, "For better or worse, old Godwin was one of my own" (209). Calling the young thug out on the balcony, Danny addresses him on the only level he understands, that of animal lust divorced from spiritual intimacy or love. Danny informs Geoffrey that his (Danny's) own wife thinks he is a "great fuck" (209) and, catching him off guard, pushes him off. Looking down on Geoffrey helplessly writhing on the gravel, he ironically thinks, "I felt suddenly sick. I could never be good at violence. Geoffrey looked at me in pained innocence. He had no idea what he had done to me, or anyone" (210). Danny's intelligence and sensitivity enable him to understand that the punk's apparent roughness results from pain and ignorance and that he himself will never fit into a world where senseless violence and toughness are the measures of survival. Turning to an astonished Godwin, Danny proceeds to pay him the compliment — "That kid's too tough for you" (211) — and furthermore shakes his hand (an appropriately civilized gesture) in response to which the professor promises to buy his book (another symbol of civilization).

Danny's narrative voice contains high degrees of sensitivity and self-awareness, traits also possessed by Ben Sippy, the narrator of *Anything for Billy*. Unlike Danny, however, Ben enters the world of the old West, where civilization disappears and Billy the Kid flourishes, a young barbarian with similarities to Geoffrey. Also unlike Danny, Ben sets out to do what he can to save Billy, destroying his ability to write best-sellers in the process. Because McMurtry shares affinities with Victorian novelists, it is only natural that he should write a story told from the viewpoint of someone who writes Victorian novels, albeit of the dime novel variety. Such a pose enables him to indulge in self-parody by presenting the effete author's desire to encounter and learn from reality versus the popular audience's desire to use fiction as pure escape. In Sippy, a wealthy, well-bred Philadelphian,

McMurtry finds the ideal comic foil for his version of Billy the Kid: an aimless, uneducated runt. Like many of the characters McMurtry admires (including the young man in "Angels near the Star"), Ben is a born dreamer, evidenced by the fact that he abandons his wife once she destroys the dime store adventure books which have made his dull married existence bearable. Yet, by so doing, she ironically does him a favor, for through his direct encounter with the boy behind the myth which follows, he grows, illustrating McMurtry's theme of the importance of distinguishing fantasy from reality. By the novel's end, Ben has become so enmeshed in reality's complex, often brutal truth that, though he returns to the quiet refined atmosphere of Philadelphia, he can no longer create the cliché driven, escapist fantasies which his publisher wants, books which trivialize the dark side of reality he has experienced.

Ben Sippy's initial meeting with Billy at once establishes the central conflict between the refinement of civilization and the wildness of nature, between thoughtful, empathic accommodation and blind, thoughtless violence. From the start, Ben, as storyteller, makes clear that Billy (like Geoffrey) is a "pained innocent," a societal misfit lacking in self-awareness. For example, the novel's second sentence implies Billy's attraction to violence is a direct result of fear rather than strength: "He had a pistol in each hand and a scared look on his rough young face" (11). Ben goes on to mention that Billy was "short for his age . . . almost a runt" and that he was "ugly as Sunday" (12). In the last phrase, McMurtry's negative opinion of organized religion is reflected as he uses it to suggest Billy's limited sense of spiritual expansiveness. For as the story progresses, it rapidly becomes ironically apparent that through his sensitivity and vulnerability, Ben Sippy is actually the stronger of the pair, as evidenced by his will to survive and his ability to appreciate life. And Ben intuitively realizes that Billy's alienation and inability to enjoy life result from his deprived background: "For there we were, by a little flicker of campfire, on a plain so vast you couldn't even think of the end of it, under a sky as huge as time. It was a place to make you homesick, if you'd ever had a home. Joe Lovelady and I had had one, but the notion had little meaning for the orphan boy, Billy Bone" (22). As early as "Angels near the Star," the night sky in McMurtry's fiction has been associated with spiritual expansiveness and the potential for transcendence. Despite Ben's genuine concern for Billy, he is sadly unable to provide him with one such moment, a moment which might transform Billy's life by giving it a sense of worth.

Ben's ability to be a constructive dreamer links him to McMurtry's positive vision of the Victorian artist as one who offers hope. In stark contrast,

Billy may be seen as symbolic of the modern novelist who cannot let go of nightmarish images of death and nihilism. At one point, Billy declares to Ben, "'I dreamed I was dead and the Death Dog was licking my skull' . . . 'I didn't have a body but I still had my eyes, and that old dog was licking my skull'" (316). In opposition to the Kid's morbid self-absorption, Ben Sippy tries to picture redemption for Billy, the potential for an entirely different fate, if only circumstances had been different:

> That night in my poor hut I did a little wistful dreaming; I imagined a better Billy, shed of all his violence, his habit of casual murder, his headaches, his fear of the Death Dog.
>
> Despite all that he had done, I guess I just liked Billy, and now that he was gone and it was unlikely I would ever have to watch him kill another man, my mind got busy and created a happy little life for him. I couldn't quite get Cecily into the picture, but I did give Billy my old skill, telegraphy. Before I went to sleep, I imagined him running a busy telegraph office some-where — in Illinois perhaps. (351–52)

Ben and Billy's ultimate fates reflect their contrasting dreams. Billy inevitable faces the ultimate humiliation (from his point of view) of facing death at the hands of a woman, a fate deemed so improbable by most that it is later ironically dismissed by all who hear Ben Sippy's truthful version of what occurred. Despite the comfort of sexual stereotypes, however, within the context of McMurtry's world, it is fully appropriate that a woman shoot Billy. For just as Ruth became a paradigm of spiritual strength in *The Last Picture Show,* so nonmacho Ben Sippy finds the strength to survive his encounter with the dark side of reality through his refined sensibility associated with civilization and with his human vulnerability intact. The novel ends on a bittersweet note, with Ben being moved to tears by a successful movie made in 1908 about his friend, which includes his fictionalized end. The ironic conclusion appropriately brings together for the first time in McMurtry's fiction the two primary sources for his own dreams: Hollywood and cowboys.

As if in confirmation of the spiritual power of dreams, midway through *Anything for Billy,* Ben meets a nun with "lively black eyes" (197), whom he falls half in love with upon discovering that she had read one of his books entitled *Wedded But Not Won.* The occasion causes him to reflect upon the value of imaginative art even for those representing organized religion: "I suppose we all — even nuns — dream of a life other than the one we actually live on this earth" (197). As Ben's words suggest, the inadequacy of this physical realm fuels the author's interest in the Victorian search for transcendence and the failure of organized religion to inspire. Like Matthew Arnold, McMurtry asserts that art can and should provide hope where traditional religion fails. For while dreams can be disappointing, even dangerous, when they become too divorced from reality, McMurtry makes clear that they are what ultimately sustain humanity, providing personal moments of faith in conjunction with reality, which themselves sustain individuals over time as they face life's hardships.

Near the end of *The Evening Star,* Aurora regrets her inability to make sense of her life's varied moments through art, as did Marcel Proust (617). Aurora's desire might be McMurtry's own and the connection of this to Wordsworth, already suggested by "Angels near the Star," reaches an important culmination with *The Evening Star*'s conclusion. Aurora's moving deathbed scene, where she holds Tommy's baby while both experience a transcendent moment listening to Brahms's *Requiem,* is notable in a number of ways. As with the scene at the end of *Horseman, Pass By,* an artist's music lifts people into a spiritual realm which offers consolation from the hardships of this world. Most importantly, the scene is the first ever in McMurtry's fiction to explicitly assert, like Wordsworth, the *reality,* not just the possibility, of such a spiritual realm from which all are born and all return. In his famous poem entitled "Ode: Intimations of Immortality from Recollections of Early Childhood," William Wordsworth wrote:

> Our birth is but a sleep and a forgetting:
> The Soul that rises with us, our life's Star,
> Hath had elsewhere its setting,
> And cometh from afar:
> Not in entire forgetfulness,
> And not in utter nakedness,
> But trailing clouds of glory do we come
> From God, who is our home. . . .[14]

With *The Evening Star,* the author dares for the first time to write in the first person from the point of view of a small baby, capturing its spiritual innocence as it explores the strangeness of this physical world which adults, until they get very old, take for granted. Gazing with fascination into Aurora's eyes, Tommy's baby spots

> the Other Place—the place where there were no Bigs. The sight startled Henry—it confused and upset him a little. He was a busy boy. He had many places to crawl, many things to bite, much to investigate. The place he had come to, where his Bigs lived, kept him fully occupied, and yet when he looked into the old woman's eyes and saw that she could see the Other Place,

he felt confused, and not happy. Perplexed, he batted at his ear or rubbed his face unhappily, as he did when he wanted to go to sleep. Sometimes he made an indecisive sound—a sound part laugh and part cry. He wanted something, but didn't know what. He tried to remember the Other Place, but he couldn't. He didn't understand the old woman, but he wanted to stay with her anyway. In his confusion he lay back in her lap and held the sleeve of her gown tightly. He let her give him a bottle, while the great sounds she controlled surged around them. Often, lying there with the old woman, sucking, he slid into sleep. When he awoke he would have forgotten about what he saw in the old woman's eyes. (629)

Like Wordsworth's golden child, Henry still has dim recollections of the spiritual realm from which he came, recollections which are already fading, causing anxiety and confusion in the process. Nonetheless, when Aurora turns Brahms up to high volume, he instinctively finds comfort and a sense of meaning in the spiritual realm the music invokes: "The sounds became the world, became his life, for the course of the special time, and he and the old woman were in them together. The old woman offered him a finger, and Henry took it and held it very tight. He wanted to stay with the old woman, and to have her stay with him. He did not want to be lost" (633).

Many years later, as a grown young man listening to Brahms's *Requiem* on a date, Henry will suddenly hide his face in his hands, barely able to endure the overwhelming sense of loss whose spiritual source he cannot remember:

Before he knew it, the music had taken him to another place—to an old place in his memory, to a place so old that he could not really even find a memory, or put a picture to it, or a face. He just had the emptying sense that he had once had someone or something very important: something or someone that he could not even remember, except as a loss—something or someone that he would never have again. (637)

With *The Evening Star,* Larry McMurtry comes full circle in his search for the transcendent. The spiritual philosophy explored in college continues in the middle-aged author who unites a baby with a ninety-year-old woman, a beginning with an ending, both extremes closest to the spiritual realm invoked by art. Clearly, the Wordsworthian Romantic idealism, which underlies the Victorian ethic of enthusiasm, continues to enrich the author's fiction, regardless of physical setting, lending it depth and grace. While modern critics, afraid of sentimentality, may be most drawn to works like *Lonesome Dove* and *The Last Picture Show,* where the focus is more sociological and the fine balance between optimism and despair most clearly drawn, the naked innocence and optimism of the eighteen-year-old rural Texan still burns in the private heart of the sophisticated adult, like a warm ember alive beneath the ravages of time and experience — "trailing clouds of glory."

Returning Home

*Every limit is a beginning as well as an ending. Who can
quit young lives after being long in company with them and
not desire to know what befell them in their after-years? For
the fragment of a life, however typical, is not the sample of
an even web; promises may not be kept, and an ardent outset
may be followed by declension; latent powers may find their
long-awaited opportunity; a past error may urge a grand retrieval.*

— George Eliot, *Middlemarch*

IN THE MID-1980s, Larry McMurtry gave an interview in which he said,

> I'm always calculating long-term concerns. I don't like losing people out of
> my life. Perhaps it's a need for security, or curiosity. Every person has a story,
> and even if I don't write the story, I'm very interested in how the story —
> how the person — comes out. You respond to the potential and to the contra-
> dictions. Most people are to some degree a mixture of creative and self-
> destructive impulses; you always like to see how the mix works itself out.
> (Orth 516)

The author's love for his characters, as if they were real, and his curiosity
regarding how well over time they have handled their "mixture of creative
and self-destructive impulses" has led to a number of sequels — *Texasville,
Some Can Whistle, The Evening Star,* and *Streets of Laredo.* Each possesses an
increased sense of urgency as familiar characters deal with many of the
same conflicts, but with a heightened awareness of their own mortality, an

awareness which often leads to greater interest in reconciliation. Furthermore, since *Lonesome Dove*, McMurtry has written three other Western novels (*Anything for Billy, Buffalo Girls,* and *Streets of Laredo*) which gain much of their power from their use of narrative voices watching a way of life — the reader's recent past — in the process of dying.

At the same time, however, it is worth remembering that the conflicts which have haunted McMurtry since the beginning of his career and formed this study's prime focus — the conflict between the individual and society, between civilization and nature, between empirical reality and the search for transcendence — all have been imbued from the beginning with hope. For, in conjunction with them, there have always been the seeds of Victorian optimism, illustrated in as early a story as "Angels near the Star." While many of McMurtry's literary contemporaries focused on the complete devastation of the human spirit, he showed how endings and loss inevitably lead to new beginnings. Perhaps no single scene captures this sense of undying hope even in the face of endings more effectively than the opening of *Moving On* (McMurtry's fourth novel), which finds the heroine, Patsy, alone "at the beginning of the evening" (1). The narrator states: "Evening had always been her favorite time of day, and in Texas, in the spring, it was especially so. Dawn was said to be just as lovely, but she had been only half awake at most of those. It was the evening that made her feel keen and fresh and hopeful" (1).

A grand retrieval from the beginning of one's own personal evening characterizes *Some Can Whistle*, McMurtry's sequel about the haunting pain of lost opportunities and the momentary sense of exhilaration that comes with the possibility of second chances. Narrated by Danny Deck, McMurtry's most autobiographical character, the novel catches up on the years intervening since *All My Friends Are Going to Be Strangers*. That novel ended with young Danny wading into the Rio Grande, carrying his first novel and despairing of his ability to reconcile his heart's link to its rural past with his mind's need to dissect it from a distance in the present. *Some Can Whistle* shows that while Danny's recent success as a television writer has been enormous, his fight to resolve his personal demons is a never-ending one, in some ways made harder by age. While the end of *All My Friends* left Danny faced with a life of compromises between the isolation his profession demanded and his need for others, between civilization and nature, fantasy and reality, *Some Can Whistle* illustrates the bittersweet result of such a life, including its pitfalls. Though tireless dedication to work brought the middle-aged author enormous wealth and friendships with famous women, it also brought the crippling migraines of an overworked brain and an ever-increasing reclusion abetted by answering machines. Perhaps worst of all, age brought with it a perceived diminishment of youthful vitality and with it a fear of losing the very imagination which he has spent his life cultivating: "Day after day, month after month, everything that I did, said, or thought seemed to be a parody of something that I had once done, said, or thought more vigorously and better" (89).

Suddenly into this safely civilized but increasingly sterile and lonely existence marches T. R., Danny's long-lost daughter, and with her his big chance after many years to have a family and discover the moral courage in personal relationships which has eluded him. His encounter with her forces him to leave behind plans for a new novel and the controllable world of the imagination he had found so seductive; instead, he must face the wildness of human nature uncultivated, unpampered, and uncontrolled.

Danny's personal struggle to find an appropriate balance between art and life, civilization and nature, is given added weight by the passing Victorian references to Jane Austen, Charles Darwin, and Henry James.[1] The references to James are particularly apt, for in the novelist's earlier repeated introductions of naive and immature American heroines to the cultivated but sterile world of European aristocrats, ironic and dramatic echoes abound of T. R.'s introduction to Danny's sophisticated world, in which plans are soon made to take her to Europe. Like Daisy Miller, T. R. is ill-bred, outgoing, and blessed with beauty and vitality. Yet unlike her predecessor, T. R. will never get the dubious privilege of bumping up against European refinement and possibly self-destructing in response to social snobbery; instead, she will be brutally murdered in a type of incident all too common in modern American life. When Danny spies her for the first time, as she enjoys a banana split, she reminds him, in true Darwinian fashion, of a "superior animal" (126) or young lioness: "the image that sprang naturally to mind was of a tolerant young lioness, finishing off a light snack, perhaps of antelope, while playing with her cubs" (126). And as he sits down beside her and tries to hold his two illegitimate grandchildren at one time, Danny notes: "I wanted badly to grab Bo but didn't have a spare hand to grab him with; the notion struck me with stunning clarity that God and/or evolution had erred in leaving us primates only two hands. What a design flaw!" (131).

If T. R. symbolizes the fertile reality of nature Danny has too long ignored, his old British sociology-turned-classics professor, Godwin, symbolizes the opposite extreme of civilization turned in upon itself and its past. Given over to drugs and late night homosexual encounters as he loiters about his former student's empty house, Godwin embodies the pathetic plight Danny might find himself in if he were to continue his retreat from the world of normal relationships; this is especially significant since this is also the vulnerable moment Danny's imaginative powers have begun to flag. Appropriately, Danny describes the first encounter between T. R. and Godwin as a "delicious Jamesian one" between "T. R., beautiful despite her terrible-taste new clothes, sailing up to the house with Jesse on her hip, the epitome of American youth, American good looks, American ignorance, American energy; and Godwin Lloyd-Jones, the ultimate Euro, drugged out, fucked out, arted out — nothing left but brain" (191).

The balance which T. R. and Godwin, when combined, represent for Danny recalls a scene in *Lonesome Dove* during which Deets gazes up at the moon and ponders how its appearance changes over time. Sometimes it seemed so close "that a man could almost ride over with a ladder and step right onto it. Deets had even imagined doing it a few times — propping a ladder against the old full moon, and stepping on. . . . For he thought of it like a ride, something he might do for a night or two when things were slow. Then, when the moon came back close to Lonesome Dove, he would step off and walk back home" (158–59). Deets's imagined ability to step on and off the moon forms a grand metaphor for McMurtry's belief in the need to constantly balance one's dreams, however positive, with reality, a need Danny is woefully in danger of ignoring. His condition is shared by one of his aging Hollywood girlfriends who admits she has fallen into the cautious trap of substituting fantasies for relationships with men because "I remind myself that the fantasies would undoubtedly be better than the realities, and I stop with the fantasies" (108). In Danny's case, even the creation of his hit television show, *Al and Sal,* ironically adds to his problem, for through it he has found a seemingly safe outlet to vicariously live the normal married life he has never found the courage to live in reality: "I was fifty-one years old. I thought I knew the difference between fantasy and reality, and I was well aware that the perfect domestic scenes my imagination had already begun to cast up would not likely be as perfect if they were ever actually lived. There might be tension and anger instead of love and fun" (36).

How does T. R. succeed in demolishing Danny's thick wall of mental and emotional isolation? In part, by behaving like a simple force of nature, blowing through the elaborate Jamesian sensibilities Danny has formed, forcing recognition. More specifically, T. R. not only accepts her newfound father's love, she demands that he let her love him in return rather than let him reduce their relationship to inertia and mutual dependency. In a scene where she confronts Danny with his passive aggressive behavior by hitting him, he experiences a healthy though painful moment of self-recognition:

> "Of course, of course, I didn't mean to make you feel that way," I said. Even as I said it, I felt those same words echoing endlessly off the walls of the long tunnel of my past: I didn't mean to make you feel that way, Jill, I didn't mean to make you feel that way, Jeanie. I had never meant to make a single woman feel that way; and yet that was exactly the way I had made every one of them feel. (283)

Some Can Whistle ends on a note of tragedy, but tragedy tinged with redemption. After presenting his daughter with a huge backlog of birthday and Christmas presents, Danny states, "As the fetus recapitulates the history of the species, T. R. and I recapitulated her own birthday and mine, a history that had floated unborn in both our consciousnesses until that hour" (229). Like those Victorians who found cause for optimism even in the Darwinian theory of evolution, McMurtry asserts his optimism in life and the continual spiritual reality of unborn possibilities even in the face of mortality. Before T. R. is suddenly gunned down by a former boyfriend escaped from prison, she finds Danny fulfilling her lifelong dream of taking her dancing, cementing in the process his relationship to her on a basic, fundamental level all his sophistication and wealth could never buy.

The fruits of T. R.'s triumph become evident when she and Godwin (the symbolic representations of pure nature and civilization) are abruptly murdered, leaving Danny (in whom civilization and nature were in conflict) to find resolution through his grandchildren. Though many earlier McMurtry novels end shortly after the death of a major character (*Horseman, Pass By, Leaving Cheyenne, The Last Picture Show, Terms of Endearment,* etc.), the author takes care in *Some Can Whistle* to show Danny's slow process of recovery. Danny struggles with guilt for a long time but manages to survive. He even manages a polite visit with T. R.'s grandfather who, ironically, once kept Danny from seeing his family. But it is in his budding granddaughter Jesse that Danny discovers a beautiful girl he can raise and help civilize without jeopardizing her personality. In her, the extremes of both her mother and Godwin, nature and civilization, find perfect balance. For the sake of her education, Danny temporarily moves back to California; later, he has the joy of hearing her long-distance reports of all the European places he would have taken T. R. had she lived.

The novel's conclusion echoes its opening in that Danny is on the phone, but this time, rather than having his daughter's call serve as an interruption to his work schedule, he cherishes his granddaughter's lively re-

ports, reports symbolic of the possibility for balancing civilization with
nature as they repeatedly connect France to his native Texas. As he listens
with pride, Danny experiences a transcendent moment which suggests the
spiritual compensation in the face of aging and loss in a manner recalling
Wordsworth, specifically his "Ode: Intimations of Immortality from Recollections of Early Childhood": [2]

> Jesse called and called; she called and called. Less and less could I follow
> what she was telling me — France had made her precise just as age was mak-
> ing me vague — but as her smart French poured into my ear, I began to float
> back in memory; in my granddaughter's voice I began to hear the lovely echo
> of the voices of all those fabulous European girls I had such fun with so long
> ago, the stars and the starlets. . . . Their voices, like Jesse's now, had once all
> whistled the brainy, sexual whistle of youth and health, tunes that those who
> once could whistle too lose but never forget. (348)

The close of *Some Can Whistle* illustrates that Larry McMurtry, like Patsy
in *Moving On,* continues to be at his most keenly fresh in the process of
describing moments caught between two worlds — past and present — moments echoing the Victorian belief in the possibility of new beginnings. In
attempting to describe such an attitude, Robert Weisbuch has written:
"The present moment is indeed dark and confused but, as in the final section of George Eliot's *Middlemarch* titled 'Sunrise and Sunset,' it is dark
only because a new era is dawning" (27). Appropriate in this regard is the
author's assertion that the conception for new novels usually begins with
his visualizing a closing scene. [3] For whether describing the young Lonnie
setting out in search of a better life at the conclusion of *Horseman, Pass By,*
or Aurora gaining increased self-insight through the pain of her daughter's
death at the close of *Terms of Endearment,* or the aging, stoic Call becoming
inspired to scratch the letters A. M. on his dead friend's sign symbolizing
the start of a new era at the end of *Lonesome Dove,* McMurtry's fiction can
be counted on to take the reader on a magical ride, transforming the ordinary to wisely reflect the possibilities for redemption in the human soul.

Notes

Chapter 1. Expanding Horizons

1. See Larry McMurtry's letter to Mike Kunkel, dated November 11, 1956, in the Kunkel Collection in the Department of Special Collections at the University of Houston Library.

2. Examples include McMurtry's 1979 interview with Patrick Bennett in which he says, "I was influenced more by nineteenth-century fiction, and I think my main influences were not American writers. I think they were probably George Eliot, Thomas Hardy, Tolstoy, and the Russians and the French. I read a lot of Balzac, Stendhal. I read Dickens" (17). And in a 1976 interview with Doris Grumbach, McMurtry confirmed his love of writers like Hardy and Eliot, whose works he said he reread and went on to suggest reasons for his preference. He preferred "a very old-fashioned novel, a novel essentially of character and theme," as opposed to those produced by modern stylists such as Pynchon, Styron, and Updike, because "inevitably some energy, some of the visualization diminished" (120).

3. This quote comes from a letter I received from McMurtry from his Washington office, postmarked September 15, 1989.

4. See McMurtry's "Journey to the End of the Road," 22–27.

5. See Ronald Sharp's *Friendship and Literature,* 4–6. The author states that "love, sex, and marriage have been the central subjects of a great variety of serious twentieth-century literature, but with very few exceptions, friendship — which up through the nineteenth century remained a major issue for serious writers and philosophers — seems to have fallen mainly into the hands of pop psychologists and self-help enthusiasts" (4).

6. In the Bennett interview, McMurtry stated, "of American writers, I suppose Faulkner hit me the hardest; I didn't much like the nineteenth-century Americans. I still don't somehow" (17).

7. See Gregory Curtis's "The Power of Polite Discouragement," 6.

CHAPTER 2. *The Last Picture Show:* The Relation of the Individual to Society

1. See the letters in the Kunkel Collection.

2. Like Larry McMurtry, Thomas Hardy came from a dying social class. For a discussion of Hardy's social insecurities, see Harvey Curtis Webster's *On A Darkling Plain,* 55–56.

3. Like Larry McMurtry, George Eliot rejected the traditional Christianity of her youth. In its place she substituted a religion of humanity based on the idea we can contribute to the welfare and happiness of others despite our common mortality (see Bernard J. Paris's article entitled "George Eliot's Religion of Humanity.") The connection of Eliot to Wordsworth and their mutual search for personal synthesis is mentioned by Barbara Hardy in the "The Moment of Disenchantment in George Eliot's Novels." In that article she states that both "were haunted by a double sense of disintegration: by the break between past and present, and by the break between the heart and reason." This conflict is embodied by Dorothea in *Middlemarch* and Sonny in *The Last Picture Show* as they learn to outgrow their youthful illusions regarding the reality of love.

4. See Charles Peavy's third chapter in his book *Larry McMurtry* and D. Gene England, "Rites of Passage in Larry McMurtry's *The Last Picture Show,*" 37–48.

5. The absence of end punctuation along with the unconventional ellipses and unusual use of capital letters are retained from the author's unpublished manuscript found in the Kunkel Collection in the Department of Special Collections in the University of Houston Library.

6. The prime example of this in *Middlemarch* is Dorothea. As Jennifer Uglow writes in *George Eliot:* "We are asked to recognize in Dorothea, and in all 'great-souled women,'. . . not their achievement but their capacity, the incalculable quality which can survive even their direst historical constraints" (216).

7. See the opening chapter of *The Return of the Native* in which Hardy describes Egdon Heath as possessing "a lonely face, suggesting tragical possibilities" (14).

8. This repeated linking of physical blindness to moral blindness recalls Hardy's blinded character Clym, who cannot recognize the source of his idealistic illusions in *The Return of the Native.* For a discussion of the symbolism associated with Clym's blindness see Richard Carpenter's *Thomas Hardy,* 95.

9. See D. Gene England, "Rites of Passage in Larry McMurtry's *The Last Picture Show.*"

10. Hardy is famous for portraying lovers who fall out of love once the object of their love is obtained. As J. Hillis Miller states in *Thomas Hardy: Distance and Desire,* "Love vanishes as soon as the goal of love is obtained. It exists only so long as that goal is close enough to be seen, but has not yet been reached" (176). Another irony involving love which both McMurtry and Hardy portray is the opposite situation of love increasing once death separates two lovers. Miller states: "As death puts an infinite distance between lover and beloved, so it raises love to a meaningless intensity of longing" (169). In *Terms of Endearment,* Flap experiences

this as a result of Emma's death. As the narrator states: "With her death he had recovered all his first feeling for his wife; he seemed a broken man" (370).

CHAPTER 3. *Lonesome Dove:* The Conflict between Civilization and Nature

1. As Ernestine P. Sewell states, the pigs are associated with Gus and the advent of "small farms for Tennesseans and others who bring domesticity to the frontier" ("McMurtry's Cowboy-God in *Lonesome Dove*," 223).

2. See Thomas Hardy's *Jude the Obscure,* 72, 490. Like McMurtry, Hardy uses language as a symbol of the vanity associated with civilization. And just as Gus's sign appears at the beginning and the end of *Lonesome Dove,* underscoring its link with the main character's tragic fate, so Hardy uses the printed word to convey Jude's doomed cultural aspirations. When Jude first receives his Latin grammar book from Christmaster, he flings the book on the ground and covers his face in despair. "There were no brains in his head to equal this business; and as the little sun-rays continued to stream in through his hat at him, he wished that he had never seen a book, that he might never see another, that he had never been born" (73). Years later, when Jude dies, he is ironically surrounded by his books: "the old, superseded, Delphin editions of Virgil and Horace, and the dog-eared Greek Testament on the neighboring shelf, and the few other volumes of the sort he had not parted with . . ." (490).

3. Charles Linck, Ernestine Sewell's husband, has suggested that there is reason to believe McMurtry purposely constructed the quote to suggest more than one reading and baffle scholars in the process. Such a strategy would reflect the author's ambivalence to civilization and his concern with the reductive quality of language. For a fuller discussion of this controversy, see "'Dove' Still Ruffling a Lot of Feathers" in the *Dallas Morning News,* February 19, 1989.

4. Ibid.

5. Following Deets's death, Call — by himself — carves in wood a simple but eloquent eulogy. When he is finished, Augustus declares to Newt, "I've seen your father bury many a man, but a never saw him take this kind of pains" (723).

6. McMurtry's sequel to *Lonesome Dove, Streets of Laredo,* illustrates Call's sad plight. By the end of the novel, he is completely dependent on Lorena and the gentle world of women she represents.

7. The importance of Gus as a positive balance between the wild, potentially dangerous impulses of nature and the restrictive forces of civilization is underscored by the world of harsh alternatives in McMurtry's sequel to *Lonesome Dove, Streets of Laredo.* In this richly dark novel, aging Call is reduced to tracking robbers for railroad barons under barbaric conditions while Lorena, now a proper schoolteacher married to Pea Eye, becomes an aggressive embodiment of the smothering feminine power of civilization and language. Significantly, it is Brookshire, the male character most closely linked with both civilization and nature, whose death is most

regretted by Call. Also significant, the pigs, once Gus's playful symbols of civilization, are now frightening mythic creatures linked with death and the world of men — until a woman unexpectedly kills one. The novel concludes on an ambiguous note as gentle Pea Eye symbolically says good-bye to the world of frontier men (represented by Call) and enters, with some fear and trepidation, the civilized but confining world of women (represented by Lorena).

8. Hardy, like McMurtry, illustrates how people who are alienated from themselves have enormous difficulty forming satisfying relationships. For a discussion of Sue Bridehead's aversion to the physical side of love and the problems it creates for her, see Carpenter's *Thomas Hardy,* 140.

9. See Joanna Gibson, "The Significance of the Child in Selected Works of Thomas Hardy," (Ph.D. diss., Texas A&M University, 1989).

10. See Carpenter's *Thomas Hardy,* 116, where he states: "Propriety in *The Woodlanders* is as potent a force for disaster as Chance is in other novels, a fitting commentator on a culture dominated by false notions of respectability."

CHAPTER 4. "Angels near the Star": The Search for Transcendence

1. As in Chapter 2, I am including unchanged McMurtry's unconventional punctuation and capitalization from the unpublished manuscript at the University of Houston Library.

2. In *The Prelude,* bk. 12, lines 208–18, Wordsworth states:

> There are in our existence spots of time
> That with distinct pre-eminence retain
> A renovating virtue, whence — depressed
> By false opinion and contentious thought
> Or aught of heavier or more deadly weight
> In trivial occupations, and the round
> Of ordinary intercourse — our minds
> Are nourished and invisibly repaired
> A virtue, by which pleasure is enhanced
> That penetrates, enables us to mount
> When high, more high, and lifts us up when fallen.

3. In *The Prelude,* bk. 14, lines 70–129, Wordsworth gives the poet godlike qualities. A brief example of this can be found in the following lines:

> There I beheld the emblem of a Mind
> That feeds upon infinity, that broods
> Over the dark abyss, intent to hear
> Its voices issuing forth to silent light
> In one continuous stream; a mind sustained

By recognitions of transcendent power
In sense, conducting to ideal form:
In soul, of more than mortal privilege. (70–77)

4. See the Kunkel letter postmarked October 31, 1956.

5. While Homer is associated with Lonnie's rural heritage, he is also, for Lonnie, associated with its gentler, humane values linked to civilization.

6. For an example of a critic who interprets the novel's conclusion this way, see Andrew MacDonald's "The Passing Frontier in McMurtry's *Hud/Horseman, Pass By*" in *Larry McMurtry: Unredeemed Dreams,* ed. Dorey Schmidt, 5–12.

7. See Mark Busby's "Damn the Saddle on the Wall: Anti-Myth in Larry McMurtry's *Horseman, Pass By,*" 5–10.

8. McMurtry, *Horseman, Pass By,* 22.

9. See McMurtry's letter postmarked December 3, 1955, in the Kunkel Collection.

10. On page 4 of Chapter 1, Arnold writes:

Religion says: the kingdom of God is within you; and culture, in like manner, places human perfection in an internal condition, in the growth and predominance of out humanity proper, as distinguished from our animality.

11. See page 5 of Chapter 1, and page 8, where Arnold writes:

But to me few things are more pathetic than to see people, on the strength of the inward peace and satisfaction which their rudimentary efforts towards perfection have brought them, employ, concerning their incomplete perfection and the religious organizations within which they have found it, language which properly applies to complete perfection, and is a far-off echo of the human soul's prophecy of it.

12. See page 8 of Larry McMurtry's preface to the 1987 Touchstone edition of the novel.

13. Ibid.

14. See William Wordsworth's "Ode: Intimations of Immortality from Recollections of Early Childhood," lines 58–65.

CHAPTER 5. Returning Home

1. *Some Can Whistle,* 123, 191, 243.

2. See Wordsworth's "Ode: Intimations of Immortality from Recollections of Early Childhood," lines 175–86:

What though the radiance which was once so bright
Be now forever taken from my sight,
   Though nothing can bring back the hour
Of splendour in the grass, of glory in the flower;
     We will grieve not, rather find
     Strength in what remains behind;
     In the primal sympathy
     Which having been must ever be;
     In the soothing thoughts that spring
     Out of human suffering;
     In the faith which looks through death,
In years that bring the philosophic mind.

3. See Bennett's interview with Larry McMurtry in *Talking With Texas Writers: Twelve Interviews,* 22–23, in which the author states, "My novels begin with a scene that forms in my consciousness, which I recognize as a culminating scene."

References

Abernethy, Francis E. "Strange and Unnatural History in *Lonesome Dove*." *Texas Book Review* 8, 2 (1988): 1.

"An Interview with Larry McMurtry." *Collage* (May, 1967): 6–8.

Arnold, Matthew. *Culture and Anarchy. The Complete Works of Matthew Arnold.* Edited by R. H. Super. Vol. 3, *Lectures and Essays in Criticism.* Ann Arbor: The University of Michigan Press, 1962.

Austen, Jane. *Pride and Prejudice.* Edited by Mark Shorer. Boston: Houghton Mifflin Company, 1956.

Bennet, Patrick. *Talking with Texas Writers: Twelve Interviews.* College Station: Texas A&M University Press, 1980.

Biffle, Kent. "'Dove' Still Ruffling a Lot of Feathers." *Dallas Morning News,* 19 Feb. 1989.

Busby, Mark. "Damn the Saddle on the Wall: Anti-Myth in Larry McMurtry's *Horseman, Pass By*." *New Mexico Humanities Review* 3, 1 (1980): 5–10.

Carpenter, Richard. *Thomas Hardy.* Boston: Twayne Publishers Inc., 1964.

Casagrande, Peter J. *Hardy's Influence on the Modern Novel.* Totowa: Barnes & Noble Books, 1987.

Curtis, Gregory. "The Power of Polite Discouragement." *Texas Monthly* 14, 12 (1986): 5–6.

Eliot, George. *Essays of George Eliot.* Edited by T. Pinney. New York: Columbia University Press, 1963.

———. *Middlemarch.* New York: Penquin, 1965.

England, D. Gene "Rites of Passage in Larry McMurtry's *The Last Picture Show*." *Heritage of Kansas* 12, 1 (1979): 37–48.

Ermarth, Elizabeth Deeds. *George Eliot.* Boston: Twayne Publishers, 1985.

Gibson Joanna. "The Significance of the Child in Selected Works of Thomas Hardy." Ph.D. diss., Texas A&M University, 1989.

Gilmour, Robin. *The Novel in the Victorian Age.* Baltimore: Edward Arnold, 1986.

Grumbach, Doris. "Talking with McMurtry." *Washingtonian* (June, 1976): 119.

Hardy, Barbara. "The Moment of Disenchantment in George Eliot's Novels." In *George Eliot.* Edited by George R. Creeger. Englewood Cliffs: Prentice-Hall, 1970. 37–54.

Hardy, Thomas. *Jude The Obscure.* London: Penguin, 1986.

———. *The Return of The Native.* New York: Signet, 1959.

———. *The Woodlanders.* New York: Harper and Brothers, 1912.

Houghton, Walter E. *The Victorian Frame of Mind.* New Haven: Yale University Press, 1957.

Kramer, Dale. *Thomas Hardy: The Forms of Tragedy.* Detroit: Wayne State University Press, 1975.

Landess, Thomas. *Larry McMurtry.* Southwest Writers Series, no. 23. Austin: Steck-Vaughn Company, 1969.

MacDonald, Andrew. "The Passing Frontier in McMurtry's *Hud/Horseman, Pass By.*" In *Larry McMurtry: Unredeemed Dreams.* Edited by Dorey Schmidt. Edinburg, TX: Pan American University Press, 1978. 5–12.

McMurtry, Larry. *All My Friends Are Going to Be Strangers.* Albuquerque: University of New Mexico Press, 1972.

———. "Angels near the Star." Department of Special Collections. University of Houston Library, Houston, Texas.

———. *Anything for Billy.* New York: Simon and Schuster, 1988.

———. *Buffalo Girls.* New York: Simon and Schuster, 1990.

———. *Cadillac Jack.* New York: Simon and Schuster, 1982.

———. "The Case of the Vanished Victorians." In *Book Selling and Book Buying: Aspects of the Nineteenth-Century British and North American Book Trade.* Edited by Richard G. Landon. Chicago: American Library Association, 1978. 87–98.

———. *The Desert Rose.* New York: Simon and Schuster, 1983.

———. *The Evening Star.* New York: Simon and Schuster, 1992.

———. *Film Flam.* New York: Simon and Schuster, 1987.

———. *Horseman, Pass By.* College Station: Texas A&M University Press, 1985.

———. *In a Narrow Grave.* Austin: Encino Press, 1968.

———. "Journey to the End of the Road." *Avesta* 37 (Fall 1957): 22–27.

———. The Kunkel Collection of McMurtry Letters and Manuscripts. Department of Special Collections. University of Houston Library, Houston, Texas.

———. *The Last Picture Show.* New York: Dial Press, 1966.

————. *Lonesome Dove.* New York: Simon and Schuster, 1985.

————. *Moving On.* New York: Simon and Schuster, 1970.

————. "The Questions a Writer Gets Asked." Department of Special Collections at the University of Houston Library, Houston, Texas.

————. *Somebody's Darling.* New York: Simon and Schuster, 1985.

————. *Some Can Whistle.* New York: Simon and Schuster, 1989.

————. *Streets of Laredo.* New York: Simon and Schuster, 1993.

————. *Terms of Endearment.* New York: Simon and Schuster, 1987.

————. *Texasville.* New York: Simon and Schuster, 1987.

Mansell, Darrel, Jr. "George Eliot's Conception of 'Form'." In *George Eliot.* Edited by George R. Creeger. Englewood Cliffs: Prentice-Hall, 1970. 66–78.

May, Rollo. *The Courage to Create.* New York: Bantam Books, 1975.

Miller, J. Hillis. *The Form of Victorian Fiction.* Notre Dame: University of Notre Dame Press, 1968.

————. *Thomas Hardy: Distance and Desire.* Cambridge: Harvard University Press, 1970.

Millgate, Michael. *Thomas Hardy: His Career As a Novelist.* New York: Random House, 1971.

Neinstein, Raymond L. *The Ghost Country: A Study of the Novels of Larry McMurtry.* Modern Authors Monograph Series, no. 1. Berkeley: Creative Arts Book Company, 1976.

Orth, Maureen. "Larry McMurtry: A Woman's Best Friend." *Vogue,* Mar. 1984, 456+.

Paris, Bernard J. "George Eliot's Religion of Humanity." In *George Eliot.* Edited by George R. Creeger. Englewood Cliffs: Prentice-Hall, 1970. 11–26.

Peavy, Charles D. *Larry McMurtry.* Boston: Twayne Publishers, 1977.

Pinney, Thomas. "The Authority of the Past in George Eliot's Novels." In *George Eliot.* Edited by George R. Creeger. Englewood Cliffs: Prentice-Hall, 1970. 37–54.

Reynolds, Clay. *Taking Stock: A Larry McMurtry Casebook.* Dallas: Southern Methodist University Press, 1989.

Scheel, Charles. "Narrative and Character in Larry McMurtry's Novels of the 1970's." Ph.D. diss., Université des Sciences Humaine de Strasberg, France, 1985.

Sewell, Ernestine P. "McMurtry's Cowboy-God in *Lonesome Dove.*" *Western American Literature* 21 (1986): 219–25.

Sharp, Ronald A. *Friendship and Literature.* Durham: Duke University Press, 1986.

Smalley, Barbara. *George Eliot and Flaubert.* Athens: Ohio University Press, 1974.

Smith, Gordon Bennett, Jr. "Sectarian Religion in the Early Novels of Larry McMurtry." Master's thesis, Texas Christian University, 1975.

Sweeney, Louis. "A Bookstore Owner Who Writes His Own Bestsellers." *Christian Science Monitor,* Feb. 6, 1976.

Taylor, Ina. *A Woman of Contradictions: The Life of George Eliot.* New York: William Morrow and Company, Inc., 1989.

Uglow, Jennifer. *George Eliot.* London: Virago Press, 1987.

Ward, Carol Marie. "Movie as Metaphor in Contemporary Fiction." Ph.D. diss., The University of Tennessee, 1981.

Webster, Harvey Curtis. *On A Darkling Plain.* Chicago: The University of Chicago Press, 1947.

Weisbuch, Robert. *Atlantic Double-Cross.* Chicago: University of Chicago Press, 1986.

Wheeler, Michael. *English Fiction of the Victorian Period 1830–1890.* New York: Longman Group Limited, 1985.

Wordsworth, William. *The Prelude.* Edited by Carlos Baker. New York: Holt, Rinehart and Winston, 1948.

———. *Selected Poems and Prefaces.* Edited by Jack Stillinger. Boston: Houghton Mifflin Company, 1965.

Index